"Attention! The liberal arts are for everyor introduce us to all the personal dimensions that encompass our lives from beginning to end. But how is this so since so much of the liberal arts seems foreign to us as Christians? Begin with this book and find the answer. Then live out a rich life of knowledge and appreciation of what makes every life worth living."

James W. Sire, author, *The Universe Next Door* and *Habits of the Mind*

~SERIES ENDORSEMENTS~

"Reclaiming the Christian Intellectual Tradition promises to be a very important series of guides—aimed at students—intended both to recover and instruct regarding the Christian intellectual tradition.

Robert B. Sloan, President, Houston Baptist University

"Reclaiming the Christian Intellectual Tradition is an exciting series that will freshly introduce readers to the riches of historic Christian thought and practice. As the modern secular academy struggles to reclaim a semblance of purpose, this series demonstrates why a deeply rooted Christian worldview offers an intellectual coherence so badly needed in our fragmented culture. Assembling a formidable cohort of respected evangelical scholars, the series promises to supply must-read orientations to the disciplines for the next generation of Christian students."

Thomas Kidd, Department of History, Baylor University

"This new series is exactly what Christian higher education needs to shore up its intellectual foundations for the challenges of the coming decades. Whether students are studying in professedly Christian institutions or in more traditionally secular settings, these volumes will provide a firm basis from which to withstand the dismissive attitude toward biblical thinking that seems so pervasive in the academy today. These titles will make their way onto the required reading lists for Christian colleges and universities seeking to ensure a firm biblical perspective for students, regardless of discipline. Similarly, campus pastors on secular campuses will find this series to be an invaluable bibliography for guiding students who are struggling with coalescing their emerging intellectual curiosity with their developing faith."

Carl E. Zylstra, President, Dordt College

THE LIBERAL ARTS

RECLAIMING THE
CHRISTIAN INTELLECTUAL TRADITION

THE LIBERAL ARTS
A STUDENT'S GUIDE

Gene C. Fant Jr.

David S. Dockery, Series Editor

WHEATON, ILLINOIS

The Liberal Arts: A Student's Guide

Copyright © 2012 by Gene C. Fant Jr.

Published by Crossway
        1300 Crescent Street
        Wheaton, Illinois 60187

Cover design: Jon McGrath, Simplicated Studio

First printing 2012

Printed in the United States of America

Unless otherwise indicated, Scripture quotations are from the ESV® Bible (*The Holy Bible, English Standard Version*®), copyright © 2001 by Crossway. Used by permission. All rights reserved.

Scripture quotations marked KJV are from the *King James Version* of the Bible.

Trade paperback ISBN: 978-1-4335-3123-1

PDF ISBN: 978-1-4335-3124-8

Mobipocket ISBN: 978-1-4335-3125-5

ePub ISBN: 978-1-4335-3126-2

Library of Congress Cataloging-in-Publication Data

Fant, Gene C. (Gene Clinton)
The liberal arts : a student's guide / Gene C. Fant. Jr.
    p. cm. (Recovering the Christian intellectual tradition)
  Includes bibliographical references (p.   ) and index.
  ISBN 978-1-4335-3123-1 (tp)
  1. Education, Humanistic. 2. Christian education. 3. Education—Aims and objectives. I. Title.
LC1011.F17   2012
370.11'2—dc23   2011049817

Crossway is a publishing ministry of Good News Publishers.

VP		21	20	19	18	17	16	15	14	13	12
14	13	12	11	10	9	8	7	6	5	4	3	2	1

For my parents,

Gene Sr. and Ramona,
who dropped me off at college
with instructions to follow God
into whichever major he might lead me
as he called me wherever he willed.

CONTENTS

ACKNOWLEDGMENTS

I am keenly aware that I stand in the midst of the gushing, powerful stream of the Christian intellectual tradition as an inheritor of other thinkers and as a professor of this tradition to my own students. I am ever grateful for teachers and professors I've had along the way, believers and nonbelievers, who have shaped me, challenged me, and provided me with the prodding necessary to overcome my personal limitations.

This project is the culmination of a number of activities commissioned by Union University and several lectures offered over the past few years. I am particularly grateful to Union's president, David S. Dockery, for his leadership in cultivating a passion for the Christian intellectual tradition in higher education and for his invitation to participate in this important series. I am likewise grateful to our provost, Carla D. Sanderson, and to Barbara McMillin and Justin Barnard, who lead our faculty development and intellectual discipleship programs.

I have participated in many conversations with a number of colleagues on the topic of liberal learning, but I would be remiss if I did not identify Hunter Baker, John Basie, Bryan Dawson, Brad Green, George Guthrie, Scott Huelin, John Netland, Hal Poe, and Gregory Thornbury for their helpful comments and suggestions. I also should mention that our entire departments of mathematics and English have likewise provided me with much to ponder. I am thankful that I work in such a fecund setting. Likewise, I am grateful to my administrative assistant, Suzanne Nadaskay, for her help in so many tasks related to my work and this project.

For the folks at Crossway, especially Justin Taylor, thanks for the patience and the assistance.

Final thanks are due to my family: to Ethan and Emily, I'm

glad that Saturdays are about to return to normal (for a while at least!). To Lisa, I cannot express fully the role that you have had in this project in particular. Your intellect and your encouragement are gracious gifts from God.

In all things, glory be to God, whose story I can only repeat.

SERIES PREFACE

Reclaiming the Christian Intellectual Tradition

The Reclaiming the Christian Intellectual Tradition series is designed to provide an overview of the distinctive way the church has read the Bible, formulated doctrine, provided education, and engaged the culture. The contributors to this series all agree that personal faith and genuine Christian piety are essential for the life of Christ followers and for the church. These contributors also believe that helping others recognize the importance of serious thinking about God, Scripture, and the world needs a renewed emphasis at this time in order that the truth claims of the Christian faith can be passed along from one generation to the next. The study guides in this series will enable us to see afresh how the Christian faith shapes how we live, how we think, how we write books, how we govern society, and how we relate to one another in our churches and social structures. The richness of the Christian intellectual tradition provides guidance for the complex challenges that believers face in this world.

This series is particularly designed for Christian students and others associated with college and university campuses, including faculty, staff, trustees, and other various constituents. The contributors to the series will explore how the Bible has been interpreted in the history of the church, as well as how theology has been formulated. They will ask: How does the Christian faith influence our understanding of culture, literature, philosophy, government, beauty, art, or work? How does the Christian intellectual tradition help us understand truth? How does the Christian intellectual tradition shape our approach to education? We believe that this series is not only timely but that it meets an important need, because the secular culture in which we now find ourselves is, at best, indifferent to the Christian faith, and the Christian world—at least in its more popular forms—tends to be confused about the beliefs, heritage, and tradition associated with the Christian faith.

At the heart of this work is the challenge to prepare a generation of Christians to think Christianly, to engage the academy and the culture, and to serve church and society. We believe that both the breadth and depth of the Christian intellectual tradition need to be reclaimed, revitalized, renewed, and revived for us to carry forward this work. These study guides will seek to provide a framework to help introduce students to the great tradition of Christian thinking, seeking to highlight its importance for understanding the world, its significance for serving both church and society, and its application for Christian thinking and learning. The series is a starting point for exploring important ideas and issues such as truth, meaning, beauty, and justice.

We trust that the series will help introduce readers to the apostles, church fathers, Reformers, philosophers, theologians, historians, and a wide variety of other significant thinkers. In addition to well-known leaders such as Clement, Origen, Augustine, Thomas Aquinas, Martin Luther, and Jonathan Edwards, readers will be pointed to William Wilberforce, G. K. Chesterton, T. S. Eliot, Dorothy Sayers, C. S. Lewis, Johann Sebastian Bach, Isaac Newton, Johannes Kepler, George Washington Carver, Elizabeth Fox-Genovese, Michael Polanyi, Henry Luke Orombi, and many others. In doing so, we hope to introduce those who throughout history have demonstrated that it is indeed possible to be serious about the life of the mind while simultaneously being deeply committed Christians. These efforts to strengthen serious Christian thinking and scholarship will not be limited to the study of theology, scriptural interpretation, or philosophy, even though these areas provide the framework for understanding the Christian faith for all other areas of exploration. In order for us to reclaim and advance the Christian intellectual tradition, we must have some understanding of the tradition itself. The volumes in this series will seek to explore this tradition and its application for our twenty-first-century world. Each volume contains a glossary, study questions, and a list of resources for further study, which we trust will provide helpful guidance for our readers.

I am deeply grateful to the series editorial committee: Timothy George, John Woodbridge, Michael Wilkins, Niel Nielson, Philip Ryken, and Hunter Baker. Each of these colleagues joins me in thanking our various contributors for their fine work. We all express our appreciation to Justin Taylor, Jill Carter, Allan Fisher, Lane Dennis, and the Crossway team for their enthusiastic support for the project. We offer the project with the hope that students will be helped, faculty and Christian leaders will be encouraged, institutions will be strengthened, churches will be built up, and, ultimately, that God will be glorified.

Soli Deo Gloria
David S. Dockery
Series Editor

INTRODUCTION

All Scripture is breathed out by God and profitable for teaching,
for reproof, for correction, and for training in righteousness,
that the man of God may be complete, equipped for every good work.

—2 Timothy 3:16-17

A few years ago, the father of a college freshman approached me with a question. His student was attending a fairly expensive private school that had retained only nominal relations with its original sponsoring denomination. He expressed disappointment with the lack of a strong religious presence on the campus but was particularly concerned with what his student had related to him about her classes and the general ethos of the campus, which could only be described as hedonistic or *fleshly*, to use an old-fashioned term.

"You're an administrator at a Christian college," he said. "Maybe you can answer this question that I keep asking myself. It follows a kind of syllogism. 'Knowledge is power,' right? That's what we hear all the time; I think it was Francis Bacon who first said it, but I hear it all the time. But what does power do? It corrupts, right? Isn't that what Lord Acton once said? So if 'knowledge is power' and 'power corrupts,' and 'absolute power corrupts absolutely,' of course, then can you explain to me why I'm paying tens of thousands of dollars to have my student corrupted? That's what it feels like. I look at my child, and I don't even recognize who I see after only a semester in that place. What is college for if all it does is foster corruption?"

At the time, all I could do was shake my head and say, "It doesn't have to be that way," but I pondered his words carefully over the next few weeks. I realized that a worldly goal, power, would always result in a fleshly education that is quite secular and selfish. Power corrupts because it is the great magneto that drives our selfishness. Whether the power yields wealth or connections or fame or leverage in relationships, unfettered it always leads down the same path: destruction.

I decided to create my own competing syllogism, starting with an entirely different premise. "Education is the search for truth" (a sentiment reflected in the common use of *veritas*, Latin for "truth," in college mottoes, such as that of Harvard). "The truth shall set you free" (a specific claim that John 8:32 makes in the New Testament). "Therefore, education can set you free" (freedom in Christ being one of the central themes of Christianity).

This paradigm possesses two distinct differences from the one with which I was originally confronted: the goal of the education and the result of such a pursuit. Truth is not worldly but rather is tied, particularly in the Christian tradition, to the person of Christ. Likewise, freedom is not found in this world but is effected by the divine rescue of persons from their selfish fallen natures, a rescue that is part of the priestly ministry of Christ. Freedom, genuine freedom that transcends the created order, may be found solely within the context of Christ-centered education rather than self-centered training.

The contrasting views of education that I have identified here are crucial to understanding the foundations of the Christian liberal arts tradition and the stark contrast it enjoys when compared against the reality of most educational approaches that are lived out in contemporary culture. Indeed, our culture is the poorer (and the more frail) because of a shift away from liberal learning in general and the Christian liberal arts in particular.

When I was growing up, I always liked Metro-Goldwyn-Mayer movies because of their iconic lion's roar at the opening. If you look closely, the lion's head is surrounded by an ornate, circular ribbon panel inscribed with these words: *Ars Gratia Artis*, "Art for the sake of Art." Next to *E Pluribus Unum*, these are the first words in Latin that I remember seeing. "Art for the sake of Art," which has been a rallying cry for millennia for artists as they have sought to balance their personal vision for their work against its practical value. If, as critics often ask, art is neither decorative nor practical in some way, then what value does it have? For artistic purists, art possesses an innate value that need not bear scrutiny from any source apart from the value that the artist him- or herself has assayed to the work.

Champions of liberal learning often repeat a version of this saying, proclaiming that learning should be undertaken for its own sake, that it has intrinsic value that stands apart from any purely practical values. Generally this is stated as a contrast of sorts between liberal learning and the vocational or practical arts that lead directly to employment. More times than not, the sense is that the latter is inferior to the former, that idealistic purity is superior to more mundane cares. This is the reverse, of course, of an opposite view of education: practicality trumps idealism and abstraction such as one might find in the liberal arts.[1]

Christians will quickly see the flaws in both viewpoints. We are more than mere human resources, finding purpose in work and business. As the Westminster Catechism answers its opening query: "What is the chief end of man? Man's chief end is that he glorify God and enjoy Him for ever."[2] The same may be asked of any human endeavor, including education. The primary purpose of education is the glorification of God. The glorification of God typically finds an overflow in the edification of his people, whether the people of faith or humanity as a created race.

Ephesians 4:11–25 describes the way that God uses the various gifts and callings to build up his people to his ultimate glory:

---

[1] Booker T. Washington lampoons common images of liberal learning with a wonderful portrait: a man "with a high hat, imitation gold eye-glasses, a showy walking-stick, kid gloves, fancy boots, and what not—in a word, a man who was determined to live by his wits." *Up from Slavery* (New York: Dover, 1995), 57–58. Washington emphasizes the distinct connection between both practical and abstract education elsewhere in the book but notably in the transcript of his famous Atlanta Exposition Address (105–9).

[2] *The Westminster Shorter Catechism*, http://www.creeds.net/Westminster/shorter_catechism.html.

He gave the apostles, the prophets, the evangelists, the shepherds and teachers, to equip the saints for the work of ministry, for building up the body of Christ, until we all attain to the unity of the faith and of the knowledge of the Son of God, to mature manhood, to the measure of the stature of the fullness of Christ, so that we may no longer be children, tossed to and fro by the waves and carried about by every wind of doctrine, by human cunning, by craftiness in deceitful schemes. Rather, speaking the truth in love, we are to grow up in every way into him who is the head, into Christ, from whom the whole body, joined and held together by every joint with which it is equipped, when each part is working properly, makes the body grow so that it builds itself up in love. Now this I say and testify in the Lord, that you must no longer walk as the Gentiles do, in the futility of their minds. They are darkened in their understanding, alienated from the life of God because of the ignorance that is in them, due to their hardness of heart. They have become callous and have given themselves up to sensuality, greedy to practice every kind of impurity. But that is not the way you learned Christ!—assuming that you have heard about him and were taught in him, as the truth is in Jesus, to put off your old self, which belongs to your former manner of life and is corrupt through deceitful desires, and to be renewed in the spirit of your minds, and to put on the new self, created after the likeness of God in true righteousness and holiness. Therefore, having put away falsehood, let each one of you speak the truth with his neighbor, for we are members one of another.

This passage speaks to the unity of knowledge in Christ (v. 13), to the importance of sound doctrine (v. 14), to the pursuit of truth (v. 15), to the abandoning of intellectual futility (v. 17) and ignorance (v. 18), all in the context of an education (v. 20) that seeks after the renewal of the mind (v. 23) and that comports with the goal of godliness (v. 24). The overall purpose of this enterprise, where the gifts and callings work together in total harmony, is the equipping of the saints (v. 12) for service that glorifies God.

Liberal learning in a Christian context is not, then, learning for the sake of learning but for the sake of glorifying God and the equipping of his people for good works. It is not merely a training ground for jobs and careers but also a proving ground for the skills that will one day be brought to bear on the unique calling and service that each Christ follower has in store for his or her life. Its goals are not bound to the created order but rather to the Creator, the source of truth and meaning, who calls and sustains each of us. Liberal learning equips the saints for the building up of the body and to the ultimate unity of the faith revealed once for all peoples and generations.

Second Timothy 3:16–17 speaks to the incredible power of Scripture to connect the theological with the practical: "All Scripture is breathed out by God and profitable for teaching, for reproof, for correction, and for training in righteousness, that the man of God may be complete, equipped for every good work." While the passage specifies the particular power of the revealed Word of God, we may reasonably extend the idea to the way that Scripture provides us with a lens for viewing the world correctly and for applying what we learn. Christ-centered learning, as viewed through the Scriptures, likewise is able to teach, to reprove, to correct, and to train in righteousness. In this way, the men and women of God may be prepared for their callings, and "equipped for every good work." Liberal learning is a tool that may be employed to prepare us for the tasks that God has prepared for us. It allows us to connect orthodoxy (right belief) with orthopraxy (right behavior). It helps us to find our place in his world. An emphasis on liberal learning is of critical importance to our era, as we seek to engage our culture with the great Christian intellectual tradition that continues to provide a fertile culture for thought and action.

1

THE BEGINNING
OF WISDOM

God gave Solomon wisdom and understanding beyond
measure, and breadth of mind like the sand on the
seashore, so that Solomon's wisdom surpassed the wisdom
of all the people of the east and all the wisdom of Egypt.

—1 Kings 4:29–30

Education is one of the basic functions of both family and culture.[1] While the vast majority of human cultures have lacked a
formal means of education (professional educators or institutions
dedicated to the intellectual development of children), the process
of passing to the next generation a culture's values, information,
and traditional roles has always been of primary importance to
the sustaining of every society.

The family was the primary place of education and accultura-
tion. Girls were prepared to take on the responsibilities of adult-
hood in the company of women, who taught them the domestic
arts. Female literacy was late in coming to most cultures, the world
of reading and writing being the realm of men and even then only
a certain portion of that population. Women raised boys to an age
where they were introduced to the crafts and responsibilities of
their fathers or other male family members. Occupational stratifi-
cation was a genuine reality for most families: daughters became

---

[1]An earlier version of this chapter and chapter 6 appeared as "The Heartbeat of the Christian
College: The Core Curriculum," in *Faith and Learning: A Handbook for Christian Higher
Education*, ed. David S. Dockery (Nashville: Broadman, 2012).

mothers while sons followed their fathers into work as shepherds, farmers, butchers, or smiths. Geographical mobility was likewise a factor that circumscribed most persons, as travel was dangerous or costly, and outsiders were not particularly welcome in most cultures, making employment difficult.

INTELLECTUAL FLOURISHING AND EDUCATION

History confirms that influential cultures have always enjoyed intellectual flourishing. The biblical record itself includes an amazing panorama of cultures: Babylon, Egypt, Greece, Rome, and many others. Every populated continent's dominant cultures have produced advancements that continue to be studied. While what we call "liberal learning" in the West is directly connected to the Greco-Roman and Christian traditions, many cultures have produced incredible epics, works of art, scientific and engineering advancements, and philosophical breakthroughs. The world has teemed with the amazing creativity and curiosity of humankind since the earliest days of human experience.

In ancient Greece, however, a new development impacted how education was perceived by the aristocracy in particular. The sons of freemen, the leading citizens of the day, were often taught by household slaves who specialized in education. These teacher-slaves, called "pedagogues" (a term which derives from the phrase "to lead or guide a child"; the English word *pedagogy* comes from this term), were more than mere tutors of information; they prepared young men to become leaders whose skill sets moved beyond the practical trades, allowing them to deal with civic matters that required more abstract thought and focused reflection. These children of free citizens undertook learning that was directly connected to their citizenship status. The term we now use to describe the legacy of these pedagogues is *liberal learning*, *liber* being the Latin word for "free."

Liberal learning, sometimes called the liberal arts (as distinct from the practical arts), aimed at a breadth of knowledge that included a wide range of subjects that trained the mind to analyze challenges and formulate solutions or to anticipate future opportunities and strategies. The Romans substantially codified their inheritance from the Greeks, and then early Christians updated the pagan approaches in ways that reflected their theological distinctiveness. In all cases, liberal learning used extensive readings, memorization, dialogues, and emulations of great works (called *exempla*) to prepare thinkers for effective leadership. The foundational outcomes fostered by liberal learning emphasized critical thinking and rational analysis, as well as an aptitude for reflective thought. In this way, future actions would be informed by rigorous pondering and hindsight analysis of past events. The learning process, then, was conceived of as a living stream connecting the past with the future through the education of the very leaders who would one day shape their eras. The Greeks sometimes called this fulsome view of the nature of knowledge the *enkuklios paideia*, the "circle of scholars" (from which English derives the term *encyclopedia*), that produced knowledge both fulsome in scope and communal in methodology. An additional characteristic of this approach was intellectual humility, because scholars saw their work in the context of many centuries' worth of thought.

By the Christian Middle Ages, the liberal arts were a fairly codified set of educational guidelines. Seven basic "arts" dominated this understanding and were arranged in a very specific order that proceeded toward the goal of higher learning. The first three subjects included grammar, rhetoric, and logic, called the *trivium* or "three roads" or "paths"; the next level was the *quadrivium* or "four roads": arithmetic, astronomy, music, and geometry. These two groupings provided a progressive sequence for the learning process. The trivium's grammar prepared students to grasp the functionalities of language itself; logic (sometimes called "dialectic") cultivated skills in analysis of thought; rhetoric combined the other two arts by training students to communicate effectively with others. Mastery of those subjects initiated the learner into the quadrivium's advanced subjects, which explored how the universe itself functioned and was ordered, with mathematics providing the primary tool for this exploration. Mastery of the physical world then led to the higher forms of exploration, the world of ideas themselves (philosophy) and of the supernatural or divine (theology). Indeed, the latter field, theology, was once termed the "queen of the sciences," the purest form of thought and abstraction.

The late Middle Ages saw a retreat of some of liberal learning's energies (though certainly less so than is widely thought), but the Renaissance brought a world-shaking resurgence of intellectual pursuits. Fueled by the religious passion of the Reformation, the liberal arts pursued a theological goal as never before, providing an explosion of innovation and thought throughout the sixteenth and seventeenth centuries. In England in particular the Christian humanistic tradition took root in intellectual circles through the work of men such as Desiderius Erasmus (1466–1536), Roger Ascham (c. 1515–1568), Edmund Spenser (c. 1552–1599), Francis Bacon (1561–1626), Isaac Newton (1643–1727), and many others who viewed the divine order of the universe as the highest intellectual discovery possible. It is no coincidence, then, that English letters saw a profusion of writers who reflected a distinctively Christian view of the world, writers such as Christopher Marlowe (1564–1593), William Shakespeare (1564–1616), Ben Jonson (1572–1637), John Donne (1572–1631), and John Milton (1608–1674). Taken as a whole, this incredible intellectual movement formed one of the pinnacles of the Christian intellectual tradition, a view that the pursuit of truth is, in fact, the pursuit of God himself because all truth flows from the Author of all that is true.[2]

---

[2]Christian humanism is distinct from secular humanism. What makes us human is our relationship with God, not our status as so-called wise men, from whence the term *homo sapiens* derives. Christian humanism emphasizes humanity's spiritual essence, not merely its mental prowess.

CHALLENGES TO LIBERAL LEARNING AND
THE CHRISTIAN INTELLECTUAL TRADITION

In the wake of secular-leaning thinkers, notably the inheritors of René Descartes (1596–1650), liberal learning struggled to maintain a connection with divine truth. For many Enlightenment thinkers, religious faith contradicted or was irrelevant to the rational inquiry of scientific empiricism. In particular, the biblical text itself was increasingly viewed as merely one of the great literary works of human culture, a viewpoint that deepened under the influence of nineteenth-century German higher criticism. Christian liberal arts education shed the first part of its identity, Christian, and moved steadily toward a secular view of knowledge before eventually leaving behind the liberal arts with the rise of the Industrial Revolution, which held such idealistic education to be an impractical holdover from a more romantic era. A fierce pragmatism that merged with a distinctly practical strain of American self-identity further weakened liberal learning, propelling the professional and vocational arts into a much-strengthened position in the late nineteenth century.

While most American universities continued to offer degrees such as the bachelor of arts (emphasizing languages, fine arts, or humanities) or bachelor of science (emphasizing mathematics or science), professional degrees moved to a new level of prominence. The more traditional arts and sciences degrees prepared students for further education in graduate or professional schools, and professional degrees prepared students for careers immediately following their college years. The liberal arts tended to move into a diminished role, part of a core curriculum that forms the general education component of a student's degree. For many students, the only portion of liberal learning left in the college experience is the increasingly small general education core.

Secondary education has suffered a similar loss, with liberal learning's more traditional subjects such as reading, writing, and arithmetic subjugated to the practical arts. Perhaps the most common goals placed on secondary education are either the production of educated citizens for a democracy (which hearkens somewhat back to the original goal of liberal learning for the Greeks) or, perhaps more likely, the production of an educated workforce for the economy. The latter viewpoint tends to produce students with a much more vocational bent, where students prepare for specific jobs. Indeed, this has been reflected in the proliferation of magnet high schools focusing on careers in technology or health care, as well as vocational tracks that provide paths to licensure in fields such as cosmetology, auto repair, and service industries, or even business.

The core curriculum's liberal learning foundations reflect a tepid view, however, of the core's origins, particularly in secular settings that eschew the former capstone of liberal learning: theology. The term *core* itself derives from the French *couer*, "heart," which is related to the Greek *cardia* and Latin *cor*. The core curriculum, taken historically and literally, eschews education that limits discussions to the head and the hands but rather includes matters of the heart: the conscience, the soul, and even the psyche. The core curriculum's heart is a kind of symbol for students' entire lives, including their minds. In this way it hearkens directly to Scripture: "You shall love the Lord your God with all your heart and with all your soul and with all your mind and with all your strength" (Mark 12:30).

Education as a whole was once thought to be a formative process that sought students' moral and spiritual refinement, which was linked directly with their theological formation. Indeed, at many campuses, the university's president often taught a senior course in morality or ethics each year.[3] The development of the

---

[3]For a helpful survey of the arc of moral development and higher education in the United States, see George M. Marsden, *The Soul of the American University: From Protestant Establishment to Established Non-Belief* (New York: Oxford University Press, 1996).

intellect was never detached from the development of the con-science. Even pre-Christian education typically emphasized a clear link between the head, the hands, and the heart, cogently arguing that a fully developed person maintained a sense of balance. The Christian assertion of distinctively theological contexts for this enterprise provided a means through which Christian principles have yielded the bulk of Western civilization's intellectual achievements since the Romans.[4]

This balanced approach to education protected against the production of morally handicapped individuals lacking in con-science. C. S. Lewis called these kinds of persons "men without chests."[5] Martin Luther King Jr. likewise viewed such persons skeptically: "The function of education, therefore, is to teach one to think intensively and to think critically. But education which stops with efficiency may prove the greatest menace to society. The most dangerous criminal may be the man gifted with reason, but with no morals."[6] Liberal learning sought to prepare morally wholesome persons according to the appropriate culture's standards.

Intelligence and morality do not automatically go hand in hand, of course. Certainly the criminal justice system has not lacked for brilliant criminals, and the need for an educational system that addresses morality has not diminished. Further, the need to place that moral development into the context of a Christian viewpoint is also undiminished.[7] Christian colleges that empha-

---

[4]This view of the West has been outlined clearly in works such as Philip J. Samson, 6 *Modern Myths about Christianity and Western Civilization* (Downers Grove, IL: InterVarsity, 2001). Indeed, even secularists admit this debt to Christianity. For two examples, see John D. Steinrucken's essay "Secularism's Ongoing Debt to Christianity," *American Thinker* (July 30, 2010), http://www.americanthinker.com/2010/03/secularisms_ongoing_debt_to_ch.html); and Camille Paglia's "Religion and the Arts in America," *Arion* 15.1 (Spring/Summer 2007): 1–20, http://arts.ccpblogs.com/files/2008/08/paglia-religion-and-the-art.pdf.

[5]C. S. Lewis, *The Abolition of Man, or Reflections on Education with Special Reference to the Teaching of English in the Upper Forms of Schools* (San Francisco: HarperSanFrancisco, 1974).

[6]Martin Luther King Jr., "The Purpose of Education," in *Maroon Tiger* (Jan.–Feb. 1947): 10, http://mlkkpp01.stanford.edu/index.php/encyclopedia/documentsentry/doc_470200_000/.

[7]For an excellent collection of essays on this topic, see Douglas V. Henry and Michael D. Beaty, eds. *The Schooled Heart: Moral Formation in American Higher Education* (Waco, TX: Baylor University Press, 2007).

size the historical triumphs and the contemporary opportunities of the Christian intellectual tradition distinctively engage culture with both the hope of the gospel and the edification of our fellow persons.

CHALLENGES IN AMERICAN HIGHER EDUCATION

In the United States, college curricula presumed a moral and spiritual dimension until well into the twentieth century. Prior to the Civil War, most colleges and universities were built on the liberal arts, including at least a token foundation in Christian thought. The first college in America, Harvard, had as its motto *Veritas Christo et Ecclesiae*, "Truth for Christ and Church"; Princeton and Brown both had very specific connections with Christian sects, as did most of the smaller colleges scattered across the American frontier.[8]

A distinct drumbeat led a more secular course for many religious institutions, even as a more practical bent undermined the liberal arts perspectives of the same institutions. For Christian colleges, however, a fairly unique challenge to their role as shapers of society came from within the religious community, with the rise of early-twentieth-century religious fundamentalism. American culture has always held a persistent suspicion toward formal education, but the rise of post-Enlightenment viewpoints and other staunchly anti-religious philosophical stances created a particular skepticism among religious leaders who embraced a conservative viewpoint theologically. For these leaders, the term *liberal* was associated with those anti-religious thinkers who had "overtaken" American institutions. In our own time, the term *liberal* has specific political connotations that create misperceptions about the content of liberal learning and reinforce the suspicion

---

[8]For a survey of American Christian education, see William C. Ringenberg, *The Christian College: A History of Protestant Higher Education in America*, 2nd ed. (Grand Rapids, MI: Baker, 2006).

that politically and theologically liberal viewpoints dominate the American higher education system.[9]

Liberal learning, however, predates all of these objections, and when it is carried out in a Christian context of faithful orthodoxy, it strengthens one's faith in God and dedication to high views of both Scripture *and* tradition. The key is the definition of the term *liberal*, and for Christians this must occur within the context of theological faithfulness. It is, however, a struggle that has unfolded throughout the history of the church, as thinkers have wrestled with the Scylla and Charybdis of paganism and emotionalism on either side of the path toward the education of the believer.

---

[9]Several studies have documented that the professorate leans left on the American political scale; on January 18, 2010, the *New York Times* titled an article, "Professor Is a Label That Leans to the Left," http://www.nytimes.com/2010/01/18/arts/18liberal.html?_r=1&pagewanted=print.

2

CHRISTIAN RESPONSES TO THE RISE OF LIBERAL LEARNING

And Moses was instructed in all the wisdom of the
Egyptians, and he was mighty in his words and deeds.

—Acts 7:22

As a fiery old layman from a fairly rural church in the South completed something of a rant against the loss of traditional values
in American society, he began to praise a particular politician
and declared, "He's a Christian! He's conservative!" While this
man never would have claimed that all political conservatives are
Christians, he definitely would have proclaimed that all faithful
followers of Christ must be, of a theological necessity, political
conservatives. His thoughts reflected a typical understanding of
the dichotomy between cultural progressives, who often tend
toward a secularist bent, and cultural traditionalists, who often
embrace at least a nominal sort of religious framework. His
thoughts also indicated a very recent understanding of the term
liberal that reflects a definition that the ancients would have found
unrecognizable.

The clash between traditional Christian values and those of
non-Christians or pagans is not new. The New Testament documents the struggles of the first-century church to navigate between
the legalism of the Judaizers and the hedonism of the pagans. See,
for example, Paul's discourse in Galatians 5, where he ponders the

castration of those who would circumcise all new believers (v. 12) and then immediately laments the debauchery of the culture that surrounded that church (vv. 19–21).

The Old and New Testaments both made significant contrasts between the learning of followers of God and that of nonbelievers. Moses, for example, was praised as having mastered the knowledge of the Egyptians (Acts 7:22), which provided him with particular power as his people's leader. Daniel likewise learned the Babylonians' best teachings (Dan. 1:8–21). In both cases, though, the tone of the passages seems to depict these activities as being somewhat unusual or even possessing a hint of danger.

The defensiveness that may arise in the handling of learning in a non-Christian context is almost like that of the Old Testament guidance on intermarriage with nonbelievers: separation is the wisest path. Indeed, there is a sense in which holy learning must be rooted in the original sense of the term *holy* itself: "to be set apart."

EARLY CHRISTIAN CRITICS AND SUPPORTERS OF LIBERAL LEARNING

For the early church, the influence of pagan learning was a genuine challenge. What could be worldlier than pagan philosophies that affirmed the power and existence of gods other than Jehovah, or literary works that contained depictions of moral sins, or even plays that commemorated past wickedness in ways that might perpetuate temptations to fresh generations of audiences? If we are called to keep ourselves from being sullied by the world and its fleshly ways, then what are we to do with the pagans' liberal learning?

Many early church fathers believed that the contemporary Greco-Roman culture of their era was too perverse to be merged into Christian culture. One of the primary lightning rods was drama, which was declared incompatible with Scripture and therefore irredeemable by Tertullian (d. c. 220), Cyprian (d. 258), and others.[1] Tertullian summarized his broad concerns with what became a famous statement: "What indeed has Athens to do with Jerusalem?"[2]

These critics, however, seemed to turn a blind eye to the effects of the liberal learning that enabled Moses and Daniel to serve as particularly effective shapers of culture and, especially, to Paul's later usage of classical pagan thought. In Paul's address before the Areopagus in Acts 17, he quotes from pagan poets Epimenedes, Aratus, and, likely, Ovid as he constructs his challenge to the Greeks to see the power and glory of Jehovah and his Messiah. Paul, apparently, saw a redemptive value and purpose in even pagan poets. As Louis Markos has noted, "The way [Paul] integrates these . . . pagan passages, which he clearly had memorized, into his sermon strongly suggests that he regarded them as pagan glimpses of truth into a mystery that would not be revealed fully until Christ. Indeed, Paul's use of these pagan verses, along with the line of continuity he draws from the altar to the unknown God to the God known in Christ, parallels his treatment of Old Testament characters, events, and verses as types of a greater revelation to come."[3]

Augustine of Hippo (354–430) was particularly impressed with this approach to pagan learning, probably because he himself had been educated in the highest order of Greco-Roman learning and had established himself as one of the great scholars of his own era. Since he converted to Christianity as an adult, Augustine faced the challenge of discerning how to exchange his own career as a public intellectual for a platform to serve God. He reformulated his understanding of knowledge, applying his unique skills

---

[1]Interestingly, a few "closet" dramatists such as Terrence remained in circulation. Closet dramas served as private edification in one's study or "closet" and were not intended for production on stage. For most of the Fathers, apparently, performances were more corrupting than the mere reading of the texts.

[2]Tertullian, *Prescription against Heretics* (Whitefish, MT: Kessinger, 2004), 12.

[3]*From Achilles to Christ: Why Christians Should Read the Pagan Classics* (Downers Grove, IL: InterVarsity Academic, 2007), 16–17.

in the discipline of philosophy to a viewpoint that derived from biblical revelation (as well as the church's emerging traditions) as the ultimate rubric for measuring truth.

THE GOLD OF EGYPT

In his masterpieces *On Christian Doctrine* and the autobiographical *Confessions*, Augustine urged believers to embrace all truth that might be found anywhere so long as it fell in line with Scripture and tradition, even as he advised the rejection as false anything that fell beyond that line. In many ways, the expression "All truth is God's truth" is rooted in Augustine's approach to knowledge.[4] As a biblicist, Augustine appealed to Scripture itself for the precedent in doing this, articulating the famous "gold of Egypt" argument that has endured since his time. For this, Augustine turned to Exodus 12, noting that when the Israelites left Egypt, they raided the gold, silver, and clothing of their oppressors and took the precious material into the desert with them. Later, the metals were melted down to serve as the furnishings of the tabernacle and, eventually, the temple itself. Augustine termed this the restoration of the gold's "proper use," redeeming it from its pagan, and therefore improper, use.[5]

Augustine proposed that *all* human discovery should be viewed in light of the incarnation and biblical revelation, not merely those discoveries that were produced by believers. This principle advanced the doctrine of general revelation, which proposed that the entire created world is infused with the Creator's nature and

---

[4]For a fulsome exploration of this concept, see Arthur F. Holmes's *All Truth Is God's Truth* (Downers Grove, IL: InterVarsity, 1982).

[5]Augustine, *Confessions,* trans. F. J. Sheed (Lanham, MD: Sheed & Ward, 1944), 113. In *De Doctrina,* Augustine includes this fascinating description of how pagan thought was redeemed by Christian intellectuals: "Do we not see with what a quantity of gold and silver and garments Cyprian, that most persuasive teacher and most blessed martyr, was loaded when he came out of Egypt? . . . [And] that most faithful servant of God, Moses, had done the same thing. . . . And to none of all these would heathen superstition . . . have ever furnished branches of knowledge it held useful, if it had suspected they were about to turn them to the use of worshipping the One God, and thereby overturning the vain worship of idols." Bk. 2, chap. 40, http://personal.stthomas.edu/gwschlabach/docs/xndoct.htm.

character, which would lead to an anticipation of the full revelation of the incarnation and Scripture itself.[6] This philosophical and theological framework allowed for the intermingling of non-Christian thought with biblically faithful learning, as long as the standard of biblical truth remained a paramount consideration.[7] The redeemed ideas were "the spoils of Egypt," which were restored to their "proper" relationship with the truth. This coherent rationale for redeeming pagan learning has yielded the enormous Christian intellectual tradition which forms the foundation of Western learning and portions of non-Western thought as well. This tradition applies Christian thought, or at least a Christian framework for interpreting reality, to every academic discipline, allowing an understanding of humanity's place in the world.

The Christian intellectual tradition is sometimes implicit in its approach, building on presumptions that are engrained into the culture or into the intellectual traditions of a particular era (seventeenth-century England, for example), but in other cases, it is explicit, directly articulating its aims as God-honoring and its discoveries as providentially guided. This approach to learning may be rightly called "devotional" in that it seeks a more fulsome understanding of God as its primary goal.

GEORGE WASHINGTON CARVER: A CASE STUDY

Perhaps no scholar exemplifies this latter view more than the great botanist and chemist George Washington Carver (1864–1943), who believed that God designed a practical use for everything in the world. This belief that creation held no wasted material guided his work on the peanut and other plants. Carver approached his work devotionally, in a way that sought to learn about the Creator by the study of creation itself: "I indulge in very little lip service

---

[6] See Romans 1:18–23 for part of the rationale for this doctrine.
[7] To some extent this paradigm builds on Matthew 15:10–12, where Christ says that what a man consumes is not what leads to uncleanness.

but to ask the Great Creator silently, daily, and often many times a day to permit me to speak to Him through the three great kingdoms of the world which He created—the animal, mineral, and vegetable kingdoms—to understand their relations to each other, and our relations to them and to the Great God who made all of us."[8] He discovered hundreds of uses for previously underutilized plants through this very process.[9]

A devotional approach to learning is only one of the ways in which the Christian intellectual tradition is expressed, but when we examine the life and work of thinkers such as Carver or other luminaries such as C. S. Lewis, J. R. R. Tolkien, and G. K. Chesterton, we tend to employ the lens of personality rather than principle. Certainly these luminaries make for interesting reading in terms of their biographies or even their works taken as a whole, but what makes their work influential is not that they were great men or women but that Christian thought undergirded their work. Biblical precepts, church tradition, and even philosophical stances guided them down the intellectual paths that produced a harvest of discovery and light to human culture. The Christian intellectual tradition is not mere hero worship or hagiography but is, rightly understood, a matter of Christian witness that points toward God, not men.[10] For example, we fail to understand accurately the leadership of the twentieth-century American civil rights movement unless we place it squarely within its theological context; men like Martin Luther King Jr. were motivated by a strong sense of divine

---

[8]*George Washington Carver in His Own Words*, ed. Gary R. Kremer (Columbia, MO: University of Missouri Press, 1991), 141.

[9]Carver's open discussions of the role of faith in guiding his research were openly criticized by the *New York Times* in a famous editorial, "Men of Science Never Talk That Way," November 20, 1924.

[10]Another effect of considering principle over personality is the avoidance of distracting arguments over the status of a thinker's orthodoxy or sinful nature. Anyone who lifts up the name of Christ will have beliefs that are heterodox in the eyes of some, including prominent thinkers such as C. S. Lewis and John Milton. In the same way, all believers struggle with their sinful nature, and we should not be surprised to learn of moral failings, sometimes significant ones, in leading thinkers. By focusing on the principles of these persons' works, we maximize the foundational impetus for their works: the glorification of God.

justice and appealed through biblically constructed means to Christ, the ultimate judge of humankind. To ignore his principles by overemphasizing his personality is to defang the very foundations of his argument.

THE GOLD OF JERUSALEM

Academia in particular has a tendency to remove the religious context of these thinkers. Sometimes this is because of legitimate ignorance of the Christian intellectual tradition or even basic biblical literacy,[11] and sometimes it is due to outright hostility toward all things religious or more pointedly toward Christianity.[12] In these cases, post-Christian scholars have no inkling that the very ideas in which they traffic derive from Christian thought. In this way, the Christian intellectual tradition may be viewed in a direction that reverses the "gold of Egypt" concept that Augustine proposed, since Western learning now bears the indelible imprint of Christian thought throughout its academic disciplines. Just as Christian thought grafted in the learning of pre-Christian thinkers, post-Christian thinkers likewise graft Christian thought into their work. Indeed, just as the "spoils of Egypt" have shaped Christian thought, the reverse, the "spoils of Jerusalem" have influenced post-Christian thought. In AD 70, Roman troops overran the city of Jerusalem, destroying the temple and looting its valuable contents as plunder. According to tradition, the Arch of Titus, built in AD 82, was funded in part by the gold and silver of the temple furnishings. In this reversal of Augustine, the gold of

---

[11]Given the basic ignorance of biblical texts on the part of evangelicals who at least assign a high value to the Bible, it is unsurprising that scholars who are now two and even three generations removed from the predominance of biblical literacy in American culture should be completely ignorant of these texts and themes, much less the impact of religious thought on the scholars of previous eras.

[12]Two dominant schools of thought undergird much of contemporary intellectual culture: Marxism, which views religion as an oppressive sham used to keep the downtrodden in their places, and Freudianism, which views religious belief as a kind of mental disorder. These thoughts and the rise of secularism in the academy have created an environment that can be downright hostile toward expressions of faith, Christian or otherwise.

the temple reverted to improper use in service of pagan or non-Christian ideas: non-Christian thinkers co-opted ideas rooted firmly in Christian Scripture or tradition and recast them in new contexts, often obscuring their true source. Indeed, part of the task of Christian scholars in our culture is the recovery of these co-opted ideas, which affirm the legitimate place of Christianity at the table of intellectual discourse.

As these ideas have been co-opted by post-Christian thinkers, the very definition of liberal learning has undergone a significant change as well. To some extent, the change has resulted from a perfect storm of sorts. The tensions between Christian and secular thought have created misunderstandings of the Christian liberal arts tradition. The fundamentalist-modernist conflict of the 1920s and its echoes across the subsequent century have created suspicion regarding liberal arts–based education. A dichotomy between the terms *fundamentalist* and *liberal* has been fostered in many circles, including those of orthodox Christianity; to be liberal is to be heterodox; by transference, then, the liberal arts must be anti-religious. This transference is unfortunate and is rooted in a genuine struggle over the very definition of the term *liberal*. Because of the suspicions cast toward liberal learning on the part of religiously conservative groups, the "Christian" part of "Christian liberal learning" was pulled away in some circles, leaving the liberal arts defenseless as they were secularized by the opposite end of the philosophical spectrum, with a new trajectory of thought that focused on the individual and self-will. Without a mooring in the faith (at least in some circles), a new brand of hyper-individualism stormed heaven and sought to replace God with the self, fulfilling in a literal sense the first temptation by Satan in Genesis 3:5, "You will be like God, knowing good and evil."

The core of what has happened to liberal learning is best viewed from a two-part question: from what does liberal learning free us, and for what purpose are we then free? When liberal learning was within the context of Christianity, the term *liberal* was intended to result in liberation from the self and egotism. The post-Enlightenment, secular vision of liberal learning exalts a freedom, instead, from the tyranny of institutions and social structures that would circumscribe our lives, freeing us so that we may follow our hearts and minds wherever they may wish to roam.[13] These answers are almost completely opposed to the answers that a defender of liberal learning in a Christian context would offer: "We are freed from the selfishness of our sinful and crooked ways" and "We are freed to return to our original purpose, the glorification of God and the service of our fellow persons." One view focuses on the self, and the other empties the self. The difference is critical to understanding what might happen in a university classroom.

---

[13]"Follow your heart" is the unofficial theme of any number of films from Disney and others, which repeat the phrase incessantly. This phrase was altered slightly by filmmaker Woody Allen, as he excused his marital infidelity with his stepdaughter by saying, "The heart wants what it wants." This quotation appears in an interview in *Time* (August 31, 1992), http://www.time.com/time/magazine/article/0,9171,976345-5,00.html. These thoughts contrast with Jeremiah 17:9: "The heart is deceitful above all things, and desperately sick; who can understand it?"

3

WHAT'S SO LIBERAL ABOUT LIBERAL LEARNING?

For freedom Christ has set us free; stand firm therefore, and do not submit again to a yoke of slavery.

—Galatians 5:1

Few pop stars have achieved the success George Michael had in the late 1980s and early 1990s. A staple on MTV and radio, he sold over one hundred million records worldwide. He attained fame, dated renowned models, and was followed by the paparazzi at all hours of the day. After a few years, however, he soured on the burdens of fame and in 1990 released a song called "Freedom '90" that included these lines: "Well it looks like the road to heaven / but it feels like the road to hell."[1] The accompanying video depicted the destruction of symbolic items from his previous videos: a distinctive leather jacket, a classic guitar, and other items. His statement was clear: I want freedom to do what I want to do; I no longer want to be saddled with the burdens of high expectations.

Michael's declarations of independence, however, began to generate other headlines, and his newfound freedom collapsed into a series of high-profile incidents. He was arrested repeatedly, involved in a number of scandals, and admitted dependence on

---

[1]George Michael, "Freedom '90," *Listen without Prejudice, Volume 1* (Columbia Records, 1990).

drugs. In asserting his self-determination, he had sold himself to a more onerous master: himself.

FREEDOM AND THE LIBERAL ARTS

From its earliest days, liberal learning has sought to inculcate freedom in the learner. As we noted earlier, the root of the term *liberal* is *liber*, the Latin term for "free." The Roman philosopher Seneca (AD 4–65) wrote that liberal learning was fit only for the freeborn citizen and that it carried a wholly moral force, which should be communicated clearly to students.[2] For the better part of history, liberal learning focused on creating unselfish leaders who were dedicated to the service of society.[3] A classic text used to illustrate this type of leadership was Virgil's *The Aeneid*, which tells the story of Aeneas, the archetype of the Roman ruling class. Aeneas falls in love with Dido, the queen of Carthage, but receives a message from the gods that he must leave her behind and sail to Italy, where his descendants will found Rome. Virgil uses a phrase that describes the calling of the freeborn leader who prioritizes service to society over the self, calling Aeneas "duty-bound."[4] Liberal learning viewed the self with suspicion rather than institutions or traditions; even a cursory reading of history provided illustrations aplenty that explained such mistrust.

The American Academy for Liberal Education provides accred-

---

[2]Lucius Annaeus Seneca, "Moral Epistle 88," in *Moral Epistles*, vol. 2, trans. Richard M. Gummere (Cambridge, MA: Harvard University Press, 1917–1925), http://www.stoics.com/seneca_epistles_book_2.html#'LXXXVIII1.

[3]Marcus Aurelius, the Stoic philosopher, battled the idea of the selfish, pleasure-seeking ego in his influential treatise *Meditations*, trans. George Long (New York: Dover, 1997), which became standard reading for two millennia. More recently, in 1946, José Ortega y Gasset wrote, "General education means the whole development of an individual, apart from his occupational training. It includes the civilizing of his life purposes, the refinishing of his emotional reaction, and the maturing of his understanding about the nature of things according to the best knowledge of our time," in *Mission of the University*, trans. Howard Lee Nostrand (London: Kegan Paul, Trench, Trubner, 1946). This is quoted in Henry Rosovsky, *The University: An Owner's Manual* (New York: Norton, 1990): 100–101. Rosovsky himself explores the value of humility, humanity, and humor in liberal education, traits he learned from John Buchan.

[4]Virgil, *The Aeneid*, in *The Norton Anthology of World Masterpieces*, exp. ed., ed. Maynard Mack, trans. Robert Fitzgerald (New York: Norton, 1997), 659–83.

itation for programs of liberal arts, seeking to preserve the best of traditional liberal learning. Their guidelines for colleges and universities note three educational goals for academic programs: "introducing students to the pursuit of knowledge for its own sake and for the good it brings to self and society; cultivating thoughtful and responsible persons and citizens, and preparing young men and women for the world of work."[5] Another professional group, the Association of American Colleges and Universities, includes a similar statement on liberal learning: "A liberal education helps students develop a sense of social responsibility, as well as strong and transferable intellectual and practical skills such as communication, analytical and problem-solving skills, and a demonstrated ability to apply knowledge and skills in real-world settings."[6]

Traditional liberal learning, then, always connects the individual with a larger purpose beyond the self. The learner seeks to pursue goals loftier than hedonism or mere creature comfort by submitting to the tutelage of the best thinkers of the past in preparation for the challenges and opportunities of the present and the future.

REDEFINING FREEDOM

The goals of traditional liberal learning, however, bear little resemblance to those of modern liberal learning. Detached from the old trivium and quadrivium, as well as philosophy and theology, students now graze according to their personal choices and preferences, unmoored from any source of intellectual authority.[7] Indeed, the issue of authority is critical to contemporary liberal

[5]http://www.aale.org/pdf/2009InstitutionalStandardsandCriteria.pdf.

[6]http://www.aacu.org/leap/what_is_liberal_education.cfm.

[7]See, e.g., Brown University's website that documents the goals for their liberal learning track: "At Brown, rather than specifying [a defined body of knowledge], we challenge you to develop your own core. Our open curriculum ensures you great freedom in directing the course of your education, but it also expects you to remain open to people, ideas, and experiences that may be entirely new. By cultivating such openness, you will learn to make the most of the freedom you have, and to chart the broadest possible intellectual journey," http://www.brown.edu/Administration/Dean_of_the_College/curriculum/liberal_learning.

learning, which seeks to free the learner from all sources of author-ity and restraint in order to achieve self-actualization.

Modern liberalism's traditions are rooted in such thinkers as John Stuart Mill, John Rawls, and many others. Its purest form proposes that liberty is the basic state of humankind and that any limitation on freedom is, therefore, unnatural.[8] In educational terms, this view of what it means to be free asks the learner to exalt him- or herself to the level of the ultimate arbiter of truth or, that lacking, preference. Liberal learning, then, seeks to free the individual from any external authority. In the interest of self-deter-minism, formal institutions and traditions are rejected because they restrict the freedom to make personal choices at will. Religion should be rebuffed as a holdover from past ignorance; marriage should be rejected as an archaic economic fetter; collective moral-ity should be jettisoned as a circumscription of personal choice, and any other institution, tradition, or locus of authority should be scrutinized and accepted only if it fits within the wishes of the individual. Ironically, in many forms of modern liberalism, indi-vidualism is tied to statism, the belief that the state is not only the best tool for protecting liberty but also the ultimate provider of freedom. This leads to a complicated view of government, which is somehow both a threat to liberty and an agent of social justice. This convolution reflects problems inherent in the curricula of modern liberal learning: a lack of coherence, deep conversations, and peace. This should be expected, because wherever selfishness reigns, conflict and bullying always find purchase.

THE CHRISTIAN VIEW OF LIBERTY

Christians recognize the exaltation of the ego as the oldest lie in Scripture, rooted in the fall in Genesis 3. The Serpent tempts Eve's selfish sense of herself by offering her the opportunity to replace

---

[8]Gerald Gaus and Shane D. Courtland, "Liberalism," in *Stanford Encyclopedia of Philosophy*, http://plato.stanford.edu/entries/liberalism/.

the authority of God with the authority of the self: "For God knows that when you eat of [the tree] your eyes will be opened, and you will be like God, knowing good and evil" (v. 5). The Serpent understood that humankind was created to be subject to a ruler, the rightful ruler being God, but in the fall, we supplanted our rightful state as subjects with a wrongful, brutal new master: sin.

The Scriptures are clear about slavery to sin: it was the virus that infected our hearts and led to the intense chaos that results in wars, conflict, and moral failure. Perhaps no biblical writer described our state better than Jeremiah: "Cursed is the man who trusts in man and makes flesh his strength, whose heart turns away from the LORD. . . . The heart is deceitful above all things, and desperately sick; who can understand it?" (17:5, 9).

The New Testament writers had no qualms about declaring sin's hold on our hearts to be outright slavery. Christ himself claimed, "Everyone who practices sin is a slave to sin. . . . So if the Son sets you free, you will be free indeed" (John 8:34, 36). This is among the most basic distillations of the gospel: once we were slaves and now we have been freed. Similarly, in Matthew 6:24 Christ declares, "No one can serve two masters, for either he will hate the one and love the other, or he will be devoted to the one and despise the other. You cannot serve God and money." Christ reiterates the image of slavery to sin in John 8:34 as well.

Paul extends this idea in Romans, where he also uses the language of slavery to sin: "We know that our old self was crucified with him in order that the body of sin might be brought to nothing, so that we would no longer be enslaved to sin" (6:6). The resurrection of Christ effected this redemption from enslavement, allowing his followers to be "dead to sin and alive to God in Christ Jesus" (v. 11). Because we are dead to sin's hold over our lives, we are not to let sin rule over us or "obey its passions" (v. 12). He understands, however, that sin's reign over our passions recalls the struggles that the Israelites had in the exodus as they constantly looked with wistfulness at their former slavery in Egypt (Num. 11:4–6). Paul warns believers to remember that Christ has set them free, to "stand firm therefore, and do not submit again to a yoke of slavery" (Gal. 5:1). In that same passage, he lists a plethora of temptations that must be resisted, ranging from indulgences of the flesh to attitudes to any action that might disqualify one from inheriting the kingdom of God (vv. 19–24). First Peter 2:16 continues this admonition, exhorting Christians to "live as people who are free, not using your freedom as a cover-up for evil, but living as servants of God."

This image of Christians' status as "servants of God" supports Paul's image of Christians as being no longer slaves to sin but slaves to the one who redeemed them: Christ. As he says, "Now that you have been set free from sin and have become slaves of God, the fruit you get leads to sanctification and its end, eternal life. For the wages of sin [as master] is death, but the free gift of God is eternal life in Christ Jesus our Lord" (Rom. 6:22–23).

For Paul, Christ purchased freedom not merely for individual benefits but also for the community of faith, the church, and even the world at large. He emphasizes that we are not freed for privilege or indulgence but rather for service: "For though I am free from all, I have made myself a servant to all, that I might win more of them" (1 Cor. 9:19). This roughly compares to a Christian version of the view held during the classical era of the citizen-leader who serves not the self but rather the larger culture. For Paul, though, the emphasis was on the kingdom of God.

Christianity's ultimate irony, then, is that we are set free from one master (sin) in order to enjoy the benefits of our rightful master (Christ, who brings us true freedom). This paradox, slavery to Christian liberty, is the intriguing opportunity afforded by liberal learning in a Christian context. Education redirects the individual's impulses away from unworthy thoughts and futile actions into a higher vision of what may be possible in service to God and his people.

FREDERICK DOUGLASS: A CASE STUDY

Perhaps a historical case study will be helpful in viewing the contrast between the modern and classical views of liberal learning: Frederick Douglass (1818–1893). Douglass was born a slave, and after escaping to freedom he wrote his autobiography, describing how he had gained the impulse to pursue his freedom. Central to this pursuit was the education he received, meager at first but later more fulsome. One of his masters warned about the dangers of providing slaves with even basic literacy: "If you teach [him] (speaking of myself) how to read, there would be no keeping him. It would forever unfit him to be a slave. He would at once become unmanageable, and of no value to his master. As to himself, it could do him no good, but a great deal of harm. It would make him discontent and unhappy."[9] Despite this warning, Douglass pursued an education, overcoming obstacles and noting that literacy "was the turning-point in my career as a slave. It rekindled the few expiring embers of freedom, and revived within me a sense of my own manhood. It recalled the departed self-confidence, and inspires me again with a determination to be free. . . . I felt as I never felt before."[10] He called this his first taste of freedom, "a glorious resurrection, from the tomb of slavery, to the heaven of freedom. My long-crushed spirit rose, cowardice departed, bold defiance took its place; and I now resolved that, however long I might remain a slave in form, the day had passed forever when I could be a slave in fact."[11]

For Douglass, a liberal education provided a critical defense against all forms of oppression, from the oppression of the self

<hr>

[9]Frederick Douglass, *Narrative of the Life of Frederick Douglass* (New York: Dover, 1995), 20.
[10]Ibid., 43.
[11]Ibid.

(through laziness and passivity) to that of chattel slavery, which deludes the slave into believing that servitude is the only option for life. Similarly, a Christian approach to liberal learning prevents the individual from being deluded into either luxury or laziness, making him no longer "fit," to use Douglass's term, to be a slave to any man or selfishness.

Christ-centered liberal learning restores right order to the learner's life. Paul lays out perhaps the best description of the aim of liberal learning: "Whatever is true, whatever is honorable, whatever is just, whatever is pure, whatever is lovely, whatever is commendable, if there is any excellence, if there is anything worthy of praise, think about these things. What you have learned and received and heard and seen in me—practice these things, and the God of peace will be with you" (Phil. 4:8–9).

Christ followers are to be agents of God's peace, wherever they may be led in this world. Their peace results directly from the change that may be enjoyed through Christ's redemption of their souls from slavery to sin. This redemption is not merely effective on their souls; it transforms their minds as well. Before their rightful Lord, they are humble, and as Psalm 111:10 asserts, they possess a holy fear, "the beginning of wisdom; all those who practice it have a good understanding." As they develop wisdom, they prepare for their personal calling from God.

4

WISDOM AND LIBERAL LEARNING

Where is the one who is wise? Where is the scribe? Where is
the debater of this age? Has not God made foolish the wisdom
of the world? . . . For the foolishness of God is wiser than men,
and the weakness of God is stronger than men.

—1 Corinthians 1:20, 25

When I began teaching freshman composition two decades ago,
the most difficult part of the course was helping students find
resources for their research. The first time I walked into the small
library of the college where I taught, I asked where the card cat-
alog was (the file cabinets that contain the individual cards that
document and locate each book and resource in the library). The
librarian pointed to a single cabinet, and I blurted out, "Where
are the rest?" She smiled and said that additional resources were
available at the nearest research university's library, about thirty
minutes away. I labored with those students to find even ten accept-
able sources for their papers. The trick was helping them to find
the information they needed in an accessible way. In fact, part of
the assignment was the citation of the source's source: where had
the information been found.

The most difficult part of that course now is discerning the
quality of the information. The Internet has produced an avalanche
of information, some reliable and some ridiculous. Search engines
and full-text retrieval services have accelerated the ease with which
one can view almost any kind of resource. Just as the nineteenth

century was the industrial age and the twentieth century was the technology age, the twenty-first century is the information age.

THE NEED FOR WISDOM

The rise of information and knowledge, however, has not been accompanied by a boom in wisdom. Despite the ease with which students may find information, some still take shortcuts and plagiarize their entire papers. Even with the new educational technologies that provide tutoring at all hours of the day and night, students still cheat on tests. Sadder still, graduates of the most elite colleges and universities in the country embezzle and even participate in terrorist attacks. At times, wisdom seems to hold an inverse relationship with information.

Wisdom is the ability to discern between right and wrong; it's the ability to know what to do in a given situation and the courage to actually do it. As Baltasar Gracián (1601–1648) once said, "Wisdom without courage is sterile."[1] Wisdom is the mark of a scholar who has learned *from* things and not merely *about* them. It withdraws knowledge from the bank of information and distributes it as a means to address the world's challenges.

Augustine noted the difference between knowledge and wisdom in his influential treatise *On the Trinity*. He labeled as *scientia* the basic human realm of knowledge, which emulates and builds upon the work of other persons, and as *sapienta* the wisdom that derives from pondering eternal things and emulating the Spirit. This concept builds on 1 Corinthians 2:5, 7, where Paul notes that our faith does "not rest in the wisdom of men but in the power of God. . . . But we impart a secret and hidden wisdom of God, which God decreed before the ages for our glory." While Augustine's dichotomy has been much criticized as being overly simplistic (and hostile to what would become modern science), his analysis certainly helps

---

[1] Baltasar Gracián y Morales, *The Art of Worldly Wisdom*, trans. Joseph Jacobs (London: McMillan, 1892), 2.

to create a distinction between a materialistic view of knowledge and one that is more nuanced in light of scriptural thought.[2] As R. V. Young has noted, "Real human learning is a matter of personal knowledge and comprehension, not a mere accumulation of facts and mastery of techniques. It involves . . . helping students to make . . . choices consciously and conscientiously."[3]

Wisdom is a crucial concept for Christians.[4] The term *wisdom* appears over two hundred times in the English Standard Version, and the biblical writers make specific connections between wisdom and righteousness (see, for example, Ps. 111:11; Prov. 1:7; 9:10). This appears to be behind Luke's description of the young Jesus as growing "strong, filled with wisdom. And the favor of God was upon him" (2:40; the description is repeated in v. 52). Luke echoes the messianic prophecy of Isaiah 11:2–3: "The Spirit of the LORD shall rest upon him, the Spirit of wisdom and understanding, the Spirit of counsel and might, the Spirit of knowledge and the fear of the LORD. And his delight shall be in the fear of the LORD. He shall not judge by what his eyes see, or decide disputes by what his ears hear."

In several places, God specifically grants someone wisdom, such as that given to Solomon: "God gave Solomon wisdom and understanding beyond measure, and breadth of mind like the sand on the seashore, so that Solomon's wisdom surpassed the wisdom of all the people of the east and all the wisdom of Egypt" (1 Kings 4:29–30). This divine gift of wisdom contrasts with the worldly wisdom that is very real but very limited in its effectiveness. Because worldly wisdom tends to puff one up, it has a tendency to devolve into foolishness. James 3, for example, asks,

---

[2]"De Trinitate," *Augustine through the Ages: An Encyclopedia*, ed. Allan D. Fitzgerald (Grand Rapids, MI: Eerdmans, 1999), 849.

[3]R. V. Young, "Liberal Learning Confronts the Composition Despots," *The Intercollegiate Review* (Spring 2011): 5.

[4]This concept is foundational to John Henry Newman's *The Idea of a University* (South Bend, IN: Notre Dame University Press, 1982), which is among the most influential treatises on Christian approaches to education.

> Who is wise and understanding among you? By his good con-
> duct let him show his works in the meekness of wisdom. But if
> you have bitter jealousy and selfish ambition in your hearts, do
> not boast and be false to the truth. This is not the wisdom that
> comes down from above, but is earthly, unspiritual, demonic.
> For where jealousy and selfish ambition exist, there will be dis-
> order and every vile practice. But the wisdom from above is first
> pure, then peaceable, gentle, open to reason, full of mercy and
> good fruits, impartial and sincere. And a harvest of righteous-
> ness is sown in peace by those who make peace. (vv. 13–18)

Selfish, ambitious wisdom likewise cultivates a crooked mind
(Rom. 1:28–29) that defies service of God's purposes.

THE WISDOM OF GOD AND THE
WISDOM OF THE WORLD

Paul directly contrasts the wisdom of God with the wisdom of
the world in 1 Corinthians 1, where he reminds his readers that
he emphasizes the glory of the cross, not the wisdom of men. In
the cross, he writes, we find a new definition of wisdom, one that
contradicts the beliefs commonly held about true wisdom:

> For it is written, "I will destroy the wisdom of the wise, and the
> discernment of the discerning I will thwart." . . . For since, in
> the wisdom of God, the world did not know God through wis-
> dom, it pleased God through the folly of what we preach to save
> those who believe. . . . For the foolishness of God is wiser than
> men, and the weakness of God is stronger than men. . . . But
> God chose what is foolish in the world to shame the wise; God
> chose what is weak in the world to shame the strong. . . . And
> because of [God] you are in Christ Jesus, who became to us wis-
> dom from God, righteousness and sanctification and redemp-
> tion, so that, as it is written, "Let the one who boasts, boast in
> the Lord." (1 Cor. 1:19–31)

Boasting in the Lord is a sign of humility, which is a sign of wisdom as well. Humility places one in the correct position to learn and

to serve, removing the ego and impatience as barriers to effective discipleship. As Proverbs 15 phrases it, "Whoever ignores instruction despises himself, but he who listens to reproof gains intelligence. The fear of the LORD is instruction in wisdom, and humility comes before honor" (vv. 32–33). Moreover, with much learning and great wisdom come many burdens, for in some ways ignorance does possess a kind of bliss. The preacher of Ecclesiastes warned his readers that he had spent his life acquiring "great wisdom, surpassing all who were over Jerusalem before me," but that he "perceived that this also is but a striving after wind. For in much wisdom is much vexation, and he who increases knowledge increases sorrow" (1:16–18). Nothing produces humility quite like experience.

HUMILITY AND WISDOM

Humility circumscribes the haughtiness that so often accompanies learning, even liberal learning. The Greeks used the term *hubris* to describe the most extreme kind of arrogance, in which someone believes himself to be equal to or greater than the gods. This was Oedipus's tragic sin in Sophocles's play *Oedipus Rex*, which was a defense of the existence of the gods against the doubts that had been offered up by philosophers of his age.[5] Oedipus is humbled before his kingdom, losing his wife, his sight, and his reign in the wake of his delusions of grandeur. Oedipus is a fascinating counterpart to the Old Testament story of Saul, who experiences a similar fall from power (1 Samuel 15), or Nebuchadnezzar, who loses his sanity before admitting God's power (Daniel 4). Moral lessons like these continue to be effective in moving persons toward a spirit of humility.

HUMILITY AND INTELLECTUAL EMPATHY

Perhaps the greatest call to humble wisdom was laid out by Christ in the second half of the Great Commandment (Mark 12:31b):

---

[5]Sophocles, "Oedipus Rex," in *The Norton Anthology of World Masterpieces*, exp. ed., ed. Maynard Mack (New York: Norton, 1997), 388–432.

"You shall love your neighbor as yourself." In this passage, Christ inverts the first part of Proverbs 15:32, challenging us to love ourselves through wisdom and then extend that love to others. The Golden Rule challenges us to put ourselves in the place of others, to ponder what it might be like to be someone else. As Leon Kass has stated, "The one choice that enriches all other choices is the choice for liberal education, an education open to us all, by the way, because of our *common* humanity."[6] This common humanity reminds us daily that we each bear the *imago dei*, which connects us together and with God.

Empathy is a critical trait for the wise to possess. Truly Christ-centered education cultivates intellectual empathy, the ability to understand how others think. For example, a student who studies engineering and is fast-tracked through a vocational training program can become a competent designer. Place that same engineer in a broad program of liberal learning, where she will learn to ask the questions that biologists, historians, sociologists, and many other disciplines ask, and when that engineer faces challenges in her career, in her public service, or even in her personal life, she can sort through options by employing a range of approaches in thinking, not merely those that derive from an engineer's training. Not only that, but she will likely have a different ability to be gracious toward others, to demonstrate the personal skills necessary to set others at ease, and to succeed in many areas of life at once.

The Great Commandment does not call us merely to empathize with our neighbors; it demands that we love God with every fiber of our being (Mark 12:30). We are to love God with our minds, and we are to love our neighbors as well, which means that intellectual empathy is a moral virtue. For this reason, learning must never be detached from community. The stereotypical ivory tower, where the scholar separates himself from the cares of the

[6]Leon R. Kass, "The Aims of Liberal Education," in *The Aims of Education* (Chicago: University of Chicago Press, 1997), 84.

world, is definitely not a Christian view of liberal learning, for learning must be dedicated to the glory of God and the service of our neighbors. Likewise, learning must be ready to tackle a variety of academic fields, filling one's intellectual storehouse with a number of ways of thinking, along with a full complement of questions that derive from different fields' philosophical foundations.

Liberal learning should never be detached from our love for God. The fall of humankind complicated our relationship with God as sin marred not only our souls but also our minds, damage that is often called the noetic effect of sin. Our intellects depend on God for the restoration of complete understanding. Learning is possible only because God has made it so, and he has done this to restore what was broken through sin. As John Milton wrote in *On Education* (1644), the purpose of education is "to repair the ruins of our first parents by regaining to know God aright, and out of that knowledge to love Him."[7] We are limited by our fallen state; like a person with astigmatism that must be remedied by a set of corrective lenses, our minds require assistance in making sense of the world and are helpless to understand God without his self-revelation.

---

[7]John Milton, "On Education," in *Areopagitica and On Education* ed. George H. Sabine (Arlington Heights, IL: Harlan Davidson, 1951), 57–72.

5

GENERAL REVELATION AND LIBERAL LEARNING

The heavens declare the glory of God,
and the sky above proclaims his handiwork.

—Psalm 19:1

The book of Romans vigorously defends the superiority of the gospel and Christian revelation. Paul asserts that the incarnation of Christ fulfilled the previous revelation of God's nature and person through the Scriptures (to the Jews) and through the created world itself (to the Gentiles). The culmination of this argument occurs in 1:19–21:

> For what can be known about God is plain to them, because God has shown it to them. For his invisible attributes, namely, his eternal power and divine nature, have been clearly perceived, ever since the creation of the world, in the things that have been made. So they are without excuse. For although they knew God, they did not honor him as God or give thanks to him, but they became futile in their thinking, and their foolish hearts were darkened.

Theologians call this "general revelation," meaning that God has revealed himself to persons outside of the scope of scriptural revelation in ways that specifically point to him as creator and toward Christ as savior. Indeed, at one time theologians referred to God as having two books that provide humans with an understanding of him: the book of God (the Bible) and the book of nature (the created world).[1]

GENERAL REVELATION AND LIBERAL LEARNING

General revelation is a theological mandate to learn the world's broad secrets as a specific opportunity to learn about its Creator. To learn about God, we must undertake research into his creation, from the humans who have a specific form of dominion over the world to the animals, plants, and even elements that fill every nook and cranny of the universe.

In most people's minds, general revelation is a watered-down concept that basically points to the mere existence of God and little more, sort of a milquetoast version of deism. This underestimates the power of general revelation, though. The verbs that undergird the concept are forceful, such as *declare* (Ps. 19:1); in Romans, the power of general revelation anticipates the gospel so pointedly that Paul declares that all humankind is "without excuse." As Hebrews 11 makes clear, Christ was the agent of salvation even for those who predated the incarnation, for faith allowed them to be reckoned as righteous in Christ.

A clear understanding of general revelation, then, is crucial to a truly Christian view of the liberal arts and to education more generally.[2] Just as general revelation always anticipates special revelation and finds its truest light in the brightness of the gospel itself, a Christian understanding of education likewise finds its fullest sense of clarity through the lens of the saving ministry of Christ. General revelation is superior to human discovery but always depends completely on special revelation.

General revelation underscores humankind's unique status in the world. When we ask, What does it mean to be human?,

---

[1]For a helpful overview of general revelation, see Millard J. Erickson, *Christian Theology* (Grand Rapids, MI: Baker, 1985), 153–74.

[2]I am indebted to my colleague George H. Guthrie for pointing out this concept.

we are asking a theological question, not merely a philosophical abstraction. General revelation presupposes a unique relationship between humanity and the divine, proposing that human understanding of the world relates directly to a transcendent purpose of divine origin. Humankind alone can face God.

WHY MATHEMATICS MATTERS: RIGHT AND WRONG EXIST

Over two decades of working at Christian colleges, I cannot say how many times I have heard admissions recruiters, administrators, and students themselves say something like this: "The Christian faith intersects most clearly in the humanities, but in mathematics, there is little difference between what a student will learn in the classroom of the Christian college and in that of [the secular school]. The best we can hope for in a math course is that a Christian professor will pray with the class and model scholarly excellence and Christian character."

I myself have said similar things in the past; however, the more I have contemplated the relationship between truth and knowledge, particularly in the context of Christ's revelation of himself to humankind, the more I have returned to the idea that mathematics matters to the Christian faith in utterly foundational ways.[3]

As Augustine once pointed out, math is discovered, not created.[4] The term *geometry* etymologically referred to the measurement ("metry") of the earth ("geo"), and all other branches of mathematics hold descriptive value. No mathematician has ever created a number; even the concepts of zero and infinity are discoveries that filled a void of information, describing certain functions that required explanation. Indeed, in some ways, mathematics may be understood as the purest language of general

---

[3]Of particular help in thinking about the Christian nature of mathematics is Russell W. Howell's *Mathematics through the Eyes of Faith* (New York: HarperOne, 2011).
[4]*On Doctrine*, bk. 2, chap. 38, http://personal.stthomas.edu/gwschlabach/docs/xndoct.htm#II.38.

revelation. Math describes the universe's properties and even its abstractions in ways that transcend time, culture, and language. While our understanding of math has changed throughout history and our grasp of it certainly changes even throughout individual lifetimes, mathematics possesses a certain kind of transcendence that is both mysterious and useful. This provides a glimpse into the nature of truth and reality as well: no one has ever created truth. Truth is discovered and described, but it is independent from human affirmation, existing apart from our understanding and unchanged by discovery.

THE VALUE OF MATHEMATICAL PROOFS

The first value of mathematics is its foundational methodology: proofs. Proofs rigorously analyze problems to provide predictable outcomes that hold no exceptions. The term comes from the Latin *probare*, "to test," though the invention of proof-based mathematics really developed with the Greeks and stands as a monument to their intellectual genius. Euclid in particular popularized the use of applying rigorously deductive logic in expounding the utter predictability of his statements. The golden age of Islamic mathematics built on the geometry of the Greeks by adding algebraic proofs (the term *algebra* is an Arabic word meaning "restoration"). Mathematicians views proofs as foundational to their discipline.

Proofs work deductively, meaning that they accumulate facts that build toward a conclusion. Sometimes proofs are called "theorems," perhaps most famously in Pythagoras's theorem about triangles. Proofs are incredibly efficient in that they may become foundational to further proofs; this is also the reason that mathematics as a discipline treats proofs with great seriousness. A poorly designed or vetted proof is no proof at all and can weaken or doom further proofs. Proofs are pure expressions of logic.

Proofs teach us that the universe, at least in mathematical terms, is predictable. This does not mean that randomness and, in some cases, utter chaos do not exist in the world but rather that consistent rules allow us to propose other rules, including scientific laws. Scientific laws are observed, measurable phenomena that may be interpreted consistently.

The language of proofs is employed in the field of apologetics as a framework for rational defenses of the faith. Proofs are incredibly powerful in declaring that absolute truth exists: right and wrong answers cannot be pushed into equivocation. "Two plus two equals four" is a true statement. It does not matter what era studies the equation, it does not matter what language or culture describes the equation, two fish plus two fish equals four fish, just as two ears of corn plus two ears of corn produces four ears of corn, just as *deux canards plus deux canards égalent quatre canards.*

On a math test, the answer is what the answer is, even if methods vary for arriving at the answer. This is why, in fact, some people emphasize comparative scores on standardized examinations in math among groups of students in different nations: they compare apples to apples in terms of content in ways that a comparison of scores on reading or writing cannot.

Students who take a computer programming course know that there may be several different ways to write the code, but in the end, the program either runs or it does not. Because the program is mathematically driven (through binary code), if it does not run, the programmer has to go back into the code and correct errors. In more frightening terms, an engineer who plays fast and loose with mathematical calculations can end up designing a bridge that collapses or a plane that crashes. In practical terms, no matter how much a postmodernist thinker (who claims that there is no genuine truth) may revel in his thoughts that there is no genuine truth, he will protest when his employer breeches a contract or underpays him. For most of us, reality confronts us at the end of each month when we look at the balance of our checking accounts.

This means that no matter how often someone says there is

no objective truth, or that right and wrong are slippery or even interchangeable, if the hearer has a strong understanding of the principles of mathematical proofs, such claims cannot possess the ring of truth. In principle and practice, mathematics constantly undercuts such claims.

PASCAL'S WAGER: A CASE STUDY

One of the great mathematicians of history, Blaise Pascal (1623–1662), identified several mathematical principles. Later in his life, however, he turned his precise thinking patterns to matters of faith. In his book *Pensées*, he outlined a mathematical claim about the existence of God, which became known as Pascal's Wager. Pascal noted that each of us faces an existential dilemma: does God exist? If we cannot prove God's existence mathematically, then what can we say about God's existence?

Pascal proposed that we think of two competing claims that are mutually exclusive: *God exists* and *God does not exist*. Both claims cannot be true at the same time, so everyone must face the choice of which claim to embrace. If God does not exist, but we believe through our lives that he does, living lives of charity and humble piety, then when we die we become worm food and do not suffer. On the other hand, if God does exist, but we deny this through living lives of sin and selfishness, when we die and find that he does exist and the Christian faith was in fact, the one true faith, then we will suffer eternal punishment for our rejection. As he summarized the wager, "If you win, you win everything. If you lose, you lose nothing."[5] Since the stakes are high, Pascal declared, accepting God's existence and living our lives accordingly is the only rational choice.

Pascal thus lays out a bold claim: faith in God is perfectly rational. Pascal would also say that this is not saving knowledge

---

[5]Blaise Pascal, *Pensées*, trans. A. J. Krailsheimer (New York: Penguin, 1995), 123.

of Christ but instead steps toward the conversion enabled by the direct activity of the Holy Spirit. The pattern, though, follows not merely God's existence but also the exclusivity of the Christian gospel, a basic claim of orthodox Christianity. Christianity believes that Christ alone is the Savior of the world and that other religions do not, in fact, lead to salvation (the same claim is made, of course, by most other religions). When someone protests that this cannot be true, that exclusivity is not possible, such a claim is undercut by the reality that in spite of how much we may wish it otherwise, two plus two equals four, and that no matter how hard we may wish it otherwise, if we only have $2,000 in our checking account, we cannot write a legitimate check for a million dollars.

Any claim against the exclusivity of the gospel, then, must be based on another rationale other than "exclusivity is not possible." Protestations against the exclusivity appeal to emotion and empathy and, as Pascal demonstrated, the stakes of the decision are eternal. Right and wrong choices have consequences.

C. S. Lewis and many others picked up on this approach in what Lewis popularized as the trilemma argument, which analyzes the claims of Christ. Christ himself declared that he was the Son of God and one with God (John 10:30–39), which means that we face three primary, nonoverlapping options for dealing with him: either he was a liar (and therefore not holy but rather an open deceiver), a lunatic (who believed himself to be God but was wrong), or he was, and is, Lord (and thus has full authority over our lives). Lewis encourages us to think through the choices rationally, to consider our response in light of the stakes of the choice: eternity.[6]

This same analysis could also apply to other doctrines, such as the reality of the resurrection (Paul even does this a bit in 1 Corinthians 15) and many other aspects of Christianity. In some

---

[6]C. S. Lewis, *Mere Christianity* (London: Collins, 1952), 54–56. A fourth option has been proposed more recently: Jesus as "legend," which means that his followers converted him into the Son of God and that Lewis's proposal is somewhat defective, especially if a high view of Scripture is disallowed.

ways, Pascal raised the stakes of theological discourse to a high level: upon which beliefs may one bet one's very life and eternity?

Pascal's Wager became the basis upon which latter game theories are built. Game theory is the accumulation of studies on human decision making, as every game is ultimately determined by choices that are made. Moreover, Pascal is only one illustration of how rigorous thinking may be applied to the Christian faith and, in many ways, how it may even build up our faith.

ABBOTT'S *FLATLAND*: A CASE STUDY

Another mathematician, Edwin A. Abbott, wrote a wonderful little novel-parable called *Flatland* that helps us to understand the differences between spatial relationships, time, and even eternity.[7] In Abbott's story, a traveler moves to a one-dimensional world, where everything is merely a point trapped on a horizon; the next location is in a two-dimensional world, where one sees only lines. When the third dimension is introduced, geometric shapes appear. This is easy for someone to visualize: take a pencil and look at its eraser face on, where it appears as a flat dot; when it is turned on its side, we see it as a long object. Move it in space and we can see it three-dimensionally, usually as a hexagonal prism.

Abbott sought to demonstrate that we are caught in three dimensions while we are alive. Just as we are able to see things that someone who is caught in a two-dimensional world cannot see, we are limited in our perspective by the reality that we are trapped in time. In this way, he demonstrated that mathematics can help us to intuit things about the larger world that we cannot fully comprehend.

These examples remind us that mathematics trains our minds to think in certain ways, especially ways that are rigorous and critical. These ways of thinking underpin philosophical discourse and

---

[7]Edwin A. Abbott, *Flatland: A Romance of Many Dimensions* (Verplanck, NY: Emerson, 1982).

even anticipate the empirical thought required for the so-called hard sciences such as physics or chemistry, as well as the statistical methodologies of the life sciences, the social sciences, and the professional arts. Likewise, music and art both include mathematics, as music is really about progressions of acoustics and wavelength, and art presupposes some kinds of geometrical balances in composition theory. Math is among the unifying principles of the universe, and Christians would do well to embrace the clarity of its methodologies.

MATHEMATICAL PRECISION

Science, rightly understood, is a rigorously skeptical activity. When I took a course in the history of science, my professor said that science typically asks a question and proposes an answer (a hypothesis) but that it should never try to prove the answer but rather disprove it. Ironically, scientific proofs result from rigorous disproof. His point was that science is much more efficient at disproving hypotheses than proving them; rare is the hypothesis, especially a new hypothesis, that may be proved conclusively. More common, and more helpful much of the time, is science's ability to unmask propositions that are not based in reality.

Following Abbott's parable in *Flatland*, two of the chief limitations of the scientific method are time and perspective. Experiments can test only a reasonable portion of time. If we were to dissect certain species of caterpillars, we would find body parts that would describe the creature in consistent ways. The addition of time, however, means that we would also be wrong during other parts of the creature's life, as when we look at the caterpillar, we would hardly recognize the butterfly that results from its metamorphosis. Likewise, the problem of perspective is a challenge. When we deal with many larger experiments about the earth or the solar system, we sometimes forget that we are actually within the experiment while it is underway, which is like trying to describe the outside of a car while sitting inside it. We are limited in our view of the exterior by the mirrors available to us. In other ways, it is like trying to take a car apart while it is being driven; the very act of dismantling it alters its state.

These limitations explain why computer modeling sometimes replaces rigorous scientific methodology. Modeling creates a data stream that carries the sense of the scientific method but lacks its substance. Computer modeling is driven by the parameters built into the programs that create the models. This means they are subject to the philosophical presuppositions of the programmers and are not necessarily objective, even though they use numerical representations of data to make their claims of proof. This means that computer models must be scrutinized vigorously using logical analysis that examines everything from the design of the model to the possible impositions of researcher bias.

The scientific method, then, is critical to the intellectual life because it allows us a means by which we can prevent ourselves from being foolish; scientific rigor establishes guidelines that work similarly to mathematical proofs: they allow concepts to build on previous work. Rigorous scientific investigation affirms that the world is an amazingly meaningful place, a reality worth exploring.[8]

As we pursue God, our thinking aligns more correctly with the reality of the created world. Righteousness and reality are deeply connected. Sinfulness produces a crookedness of mind that produces further sinfulness, but righteousness produces "the mind of Christ" (1 Cor. 2:16). Math works because it is rooted in God's revelation of himself, which means that it is difficult to co-opt by those who would insist that truth is relative or that the world is utterly random.

---

[8]For a more complete exploration of the concept, see Abraham Kuyper, *Wisdom and Wonder: Common Grace in Science and Art*, trans. Nelson D. Kloosterman, ed. Jordan J. Ballor and Stephen J. Grabill (Grand Rapids, MI: Christian's Library Press, 2011).

The scientific method, building on mathematics, employs proofs to explore the predictability and orderliness of the world. Likewise, the scientific method demands rigorous analysis of observable data. Indeed, the combination of these two things, predictability and analysis of observed data, are its twin foundations. This means that a somewhat clear line exists between what science can demonstrate and what it cannot. Those who would have us believe that the universe arose from nothingness that willed itself into *somethingness* face twin challenges: how can it be predictable if it will not happen again, and how can it be measured if it cannot be observed? What this means is that the origin of the universe is not a question of the scientific method but rather of philosophy, and as such, it demands to be understood as philosophy and not as science.

Faith and science, then, do not conflict, but theological and materialistic philosophies do. The scientific method produces data that must be interpreted, and the two philosophical approaches contrast. Materialism proposes that only the material world is measurable and therefore real; there is nothing reliable (or worthy of discussion) beyond that which is measurable through current means. Theology, however, not only believes in the measurability of the material world but interprets that reality through the revealed truth of the Creator of reality. A materialist, then, views the Scriptures as a cultural artifact lacking in supernatural authority or worth, while a theologian with a high view of Scripture views the Bible's accounts of history as products of the special revelation of God to his creation in order to effect a relationship with humankind. A materialist will likewise interpret the Scriptures through the lens of culture, granting the culture's values the position of authority over the Bible and following an ever-changing set of ethics and values. On the other hand, an orthodox Christian theologian will elevate the Scriptures as authoritative over culture, yielding a remarkably consistent view of the world by the light of Christian history and tradition. A materialist will say that the Bible's views on a topic such as marriage hold no authority and are merely descriptive of past millennia's cultures, while a faithful theologian will counter that the Bible is revealed truth and therefore is prescriptive for all times and all cultures, including our own. The ultimate questions are fairly simple: Do we trust human discovery, or do we trust God's self-revelation? Do humans get to determine right and wrong, and reality, or does God? These questions hearken back to the original temptation offered to Adam and Eve in the garden: "For God knows that when you eat of [the fruit tree] your eyes will be opened, and you will be like God, knowing good and evil" (Gen. 3:5).

SCIENCE IN THE CONTEXT OF OTHER DISCIPLINES

Scientific pursuits must never become detached from other disciplines, particularly ethics. Science is the best means we have in telling us what we can do, as it describes the mechanisms of the physical world (e.g., we can study chemicals and design drugs that can cause our bodies to undergo changes).[9] The scientific method, however, is ill-equipped to tell us what we *may* do in terms of ethics or practicality (is it ethical to use a drug to end the life of a person who is suffering from depression or to terminate a pregnancy?). Moreover, science as a discipline is completely unable to tell us what we *must* do (must we force a patient to undergo a drug treatment that can save a life but that the patient does not want?). Rightly understood, science is a tool, not a philosophical system.

One final point about mathematics should be made: the use of math as a kind of language to describe the world. Galileo apparently believed that mathematics was the inspired language of God's book of nature. Because of the ability of mathematical

---

[9]For a helpful overview of the scientific enterprise in the context of biblical theology, see Tim Morris and Don Petcher, *Science and Grace: God's Reign in the Natural Sciences* (Wheaton, IL: Crossway, 2006).

terms to transcend human language, we may move beyond particular eras and cultures in our exploration of the world's characteristics. Moreover, mathematics is independent from language or geography in the same way that other intellectual pursuits are. Research in biology and chemistry is dependent on the availability of specimens or resources that are geographically dependent. Philosophy is deeply handicapped by the vagaries of language. Mathematics, though, is the closest approximation of purely symbolic language that exists in the human experience. This is why the Voyager Mission of 1977 used mathematical codings as a means of anticipating communication with intelligent nonhuman species, should such first contact be made.

By examining the mathematical principles that undergird the world and that demonstrate certain predictabilities of the natural world, we gain insight into the very particular nature of God. Similarly, when we view math as a kind of language that allows humans to communicate concepts about the world in particular ways, we are reminded of a truth that stands behind language as well: words have meanings.

WHY LITERATURE MATTERS: STORIES HAVE MEANING

When old friends gather over a meal, they tend to talk about the old days. When families celebrate holidays, they swap memories of previous times. Cultures have stories that pass along their values and ideals. Stories, more generally called "narratives," possess a significant power in the realm of human culture. They move us and inspire us; they instruct and admonish us. Someone who wants to study ancient Aztec culture can gain information and insights by reading the *Popul Vuh,* just as someone who wants to understand the Mande culture can read *The Epic of Son-Jara.* These stories tell us how these civilizations defined what it meant to be a man or a woman in those contexts, what they thought about the supernatural and the natural world, and many other things.

Genesis never offers a depiction of the origin of language. God speaks from the opening "Let there be" (1:3). The Tower of Babel (Genesis 11) explains why so many languages exist but does not account for language itself. The same could be said for story: the Bible begins with narrative and presumes a narrative value to its words throughout the entirety of the scriptural record. Just as mathematics "works" for no apparent reason that may be explained in human terms, narrative also works in ways that we cannot understand apart from an explanation that transcends the human experience. This explains, perhaps, why cultures connect the supernatural with many theories about the origin of writing and language.

Narratives bind us together. When we share stories, we share life; as C. S. Lewis is often ascribed as noting, "We read to know we are not alone." Narratives help us to articulate our feelings, our anxieties, and our understandings. Moreover, literature introduces us to the great thinkers of the past, along with the great ideals of the ages and the most exemplary characters. In all of these things, we learn about ourselves.

Meaning is a powerful reminder of the communal nature of all intellectual activities. As John Donne once observed, "No man is an island," and nowhere is this more true than in the world of ideas.[10] Unless we are willing to ascribe to the viewpoint of solipsism (an extreme form of egocentrism where nothing exists in the universe apart from the self), we have to admit that meaning is all about connection. The storyteller has a point to make through the story and crafts it in a way that attempts to communicate with the audience. Storytelling presumes connection; we all know what we think about a person who stands by himself rambling on about

---

[10]John Donne, "Meditation 17," in *Seventeenth-Century Prose and Poetry*, 2nd ed., ed. Alexander M. Witherspoon and Frank J. Warnke (Fort Worth, TX: Harcourt Brace Jovanovich, 1991), 68–69.

something without an audience; we assume that he is mentally ill. A storyteller who spins a yarn without consideration of the audience is really just a babbler.

MEANING MATTERS

Meaning is a two-way street. Just as the storyteller has a point, the audience has its own presuppositions about how to interpret the story. These various presuppositions form the foundations of the various schools of literary criticism that exist. By this we mean that stories possess not only literal meaning but also figurative meaning. The story of Jack and Jill, for example, is a quirky little tale about a boy and a girl who strike out to find some water for their pail. The meaning of the tale, however, is up for debate. The various schools of literary interpretation will assert various (and sometimes competing) ways of reading the story, each based on its interpretive presuppositions. A Marxist, for example, will try to find a meaning that involves the control of resources and the oppression of the common person (Jack and Jill cannot access the water unless they pay obeisance to those who live at the top of the hill and are tossed away by those unnamed oppressors). A Freudian may say that the story is a thinly veiled parable about sex. A patristic will read the story as an allegorical retelling of a biblical passage, such as that of Adam and Eve. Because we do not have a known author, we cannot seek after authorial intent, so we cannot appeal to that source for meaning. Meaning contains a good deal of flexibility but it also defies utter randomness. Meaning may be elastic or even unclear, but it is not chaotic.

The ultimate question of meaning is where does the ultimate authority of interpretation reside, with the storyteller or with the audience? Contemporary criticism has used a concept called "the intentional fallacy" to usurp the storyteller's authority. This fallacy proposes that the audience cannot infer an author's intended meaning because it is outside of the text itself. If reading this sentence, "The quick fox jumped over the barn," the audience cannot grant an unknown author any sense of authority because the text is the only thing that is knowable. Even if we know the author, we must ask how truthful a stated authority may be: if the author says that the sentence is actually about the attack of a shark on a beach in Australia, we must question the honesty or skill (or sanity!) of the author. In a sense, when the authority is placed in the mind of the audience, it treats the text as though it had spontaneously arisen out of nothing.

The problem with such an interpretive paradigm, however, is that the interpreter may be untruthful too. Just because an interpreter believes that the aforementioned sentence means "the prom is on Thursday night" does not mean that it does. Such a reading would be totally idiosyncratic and would lack any sense of true authority. One of the problems in contemporary literary theory is that the reader (or "interpretive communities," to use Stanley Fish's term[11]) has claimed authority over both the author and the text. Those who are familiar with the story about Satan's fall from his place of power in heaven will recognize the pattern: Satan, an archangel serving God, decided to pull God from the throne of heaven and supplant him with his own leadership. After gathering forces for a celestial war, Satan storms heaven but is defeated and is cast out of the high places, becoming instead the wan lord of the material world. Interpreters who replace the intent of the author with the interpretation of the audience have likewise stormed heaven, asserting their own authority over that of the ones who have actually created the stories. It is an act of incredible hubris.

THE PURSUIT OF MEANING: HERMENEUTICS

Interpretation is also called "hermeneutics," and a Christ-centered hermeneutic seeks to connect the storyteller with the audience,

---

[11] *Is There a Text in This Class? The Authority of Interpretive Communities* (Cambridge, MA: Harvard University Press, 1982).

using the story as the medium of communication.[12] Alan Jacobs calls this the "hermeneutics of love," where the audience invokes the Golden Rule, that we love others as we would have them love us.[13] We should interpret meaning as we wish that others would interpret our own meaning. Scott Huelin calls this the "hermeneutics of hospitality," where we seek to be hospitable in our interpretations.[14] I prefer the phrase the "hermeneutics of optimism," where we seek to find the best possible interpretation, the one that seeks to find the most fulsome meaning possible based on our knowledge of the author and of the author's entire corpus of stories.[15]

Interpretation is difficult, but this is easily explained by the fall of humankind and the subsequent fall of language at Babel. We no longer enjoy full community with one another; just as our relationships have been damaged by sin, our abilities to communicate with one another have likewise been damaged. Our words are inefficient; our phrases are ambiguous; our points are muddled.

Postmodernists and deconstructionists, who propose that words cannot carry value, explore this fault line. These critics exploit the chinks in language, asking us to amplify these problems into an overarching sense of meaninglessness to all things literary. How do we define Jack and Jill's hill? How high is a hill before it becomes a mountain? Why are they going to fetch water from the top of a hill? What size of pail are they carrying? Why do we even care?

The problem with this approach to narrative is that it critiques the problems of language and attacks the very possibility of

---

[12]Three resources are indispensible for considering Christian hermeneutics: Grant R. Osborne, *The Hermeneutical Spiral: A Comprehensive Introduction to Biblical Interpretation*, rev. and exp. ed. (Downers Grove, IL: IVP Academic, 2006); Kevin J. Vanhoozer, *Is There a Meaning in This Text? The Bible, the Reader, and the Morality of Literary Knowledge* (Grand Rapids, MI: Zondervan, 1998); and James K. A. Smith, *Who's Afraid of Postmodernism? Taking Derrida, Lyotard, and Foucalt to Church* (Grand Rapids, MI: Baker Academic, 2006).

[13]*A Theology of Reading: The Hermeneutics of Love* (Cambridge, MA: Westview, 2001).

[14]"Peregrination, Hermeneutics, Hospitality: On the Way to a Theologically Informed General Hermeneutics," *Literature and Theology* 22 (2008): 223–36.

[15]*God as Author: A Biblical Approach to Narrative* (Nashville: Broadman Academic, 2010), 28–34.

meaning even while using language to make its point. At its base, then, these kinds of attacks on meaning lack self-awareness at best and are hypocritical at worst. They are logical parallels to the philosopher who says, "All rules have exceptions." Either that statement is false or else (as Pascal taught us) it is self-contradictory.

STORIES AS CONNECTION

Stories communicate or else they are not stories. Literature reaches beyond the individual, creating a connection between the author and the audience. The broken nature of language explains why meaning can be so elusive and even controversial. What it cannot explain, however, is why meaning even exists.

For Christians, though, we understand that Christ seeks to reconcile all things, including our stories. The Spirit himself is even involved in this, notably in prayer, where he intercedes for us with groanings that transcend words (Rom. 8:26). Perhaps general revelation likewise teaches us that God is at work even in our stories. As Gustav Freytag noted, stories all seem to include action that rises toward a conflict or climax before falling into a state of resolution.[16] We all seem to crave resolution, in fact, and when it is not present, we lament it deeply. For example, just ponder how frustrating it is to realize that a television show is about "to be continued"!

For Christians, narrative is particularly important because it is how we comprehend God's fullest revelation of himself, through Scripture's record of the incarnation of Jesus Christ. The Bible rightly may be called "God's Story," with all of the Bible's stories communicating the overarching story of God's love for us.[17]

---

[16]For an overview of Freytag, Aristotle, and other structural theorists, see ibid., 87–107.

[17]This is the basis for the current movement in biblical storying, which emphasizes the connectivity of narrative in the communication of the gospel. See, e.g., Avery T. Willis Jr. and Mark Snowden, *Truth That Sticks: How to Communicate Velcro Truth in a Teflon World* (Colorado Springs, CO: NavPress, 2010). When we call the Scriptures "stories," we are not calling them false or fictional; just the opposite, we are saying that they are inspired revelations from God expressed in ways that resonate particularly with humans, employing different genres for different purposes (prose as opposed to poetry or other genres). They are true even as they are powerfully effective.

Narratives possess meaning because they are endowed with meaning by their very nature, and that nature, I would propose, is rooted in their relationship with God's self-revelation. When God chose to reveal himself to humans, he did so by unfolding the story of his love through the Scriptures, which are powerful stories. This means that all human stories have a power that echoes the most powerful story ever told: that of God's love for us.

SCIENCE AND MEANING

Just as stories have meaning, however, so does the data that we use to employ the scientific method. Science only works because the universe has meaning built into it; otherwise we could not understand it. We use science to explore the world, which means that science presumes that meaning exists and may be captured in a cogent sense. When we say, "Does the earth revolve around the sun or vice versa?," we presume that research that will generate data that may answer the question. While the interpretations of the data may differ, there still are data and there still is a world of meaning that may be researched. Indeed, the very fact that we can do research means that the universe is naturally meaningful; the scientific method works only in such a world.[18]

The parallels between narrative and scientific data, then, share another issue: the interpretation of their means of communicating their descriptions of life and the world. Just as the interpretation of narrative presupposes certain interpretive elements, the interpretation of scientific data likewise presupposes certain philosophical frameworks.

When I took botany, for example, we learned how to examine the structures of plants so that we could identify the various species that appeared on our tests and quizzes. Our professor

---

[18]For a fascinating exploration of the connections between science, literature, and art, see Benjamin Wiker and Jonathan Witt, *A Meaningful World: How the Arts and Sciences Reveal the Genius of Nature* (Downers Grove, IL: IVP Academic, 2006).

taught us to look at leaves, for example, and to identify certain categories. In an offhand comment, he noted that the broad categories indicated the shared ancestry of the various species. His comment was a reflection of his hermeneutical lens that caused him to see the data in that way. For someone else who is guided by a belief in a designer, the common elements and similarities may be viewed as indicators of a shared creator, whose characteristics are just as distinctive and common as the brushstrokes of a particular Japanese watercolor painter or the repeated patterns of Warhol's prints. The data themselves do not drive the interpretation; the interpreter's understanding of the world generates the interpretation.

Much of the perceived conflict between faith and science is really an issue of data hermeneutics. Scientific materialism treats the universe in much the same way as literary critics detach text from authorial intent. If the universe has no author, then it has no intentionality, which means that its meaning is found only in the minds of its interpreters, those who analyze scientific data. The intentional fallacy that has afflicted much of literary criticism is shared by those who subscribe to a scientific viewpoint that there is no intentionality to the universe either. If the universe is random, it has no meaning. If it has no meaning, it has no originator of meaning. All authority, then, is ceded to the interpreters: scientific materialists. If the world *has* meaning, then it is only logical that is has an *originator* of that meaning; without an originator, there is no source of meaning. Or meaningful data. If the world is meaningful, then by definition it cannot be random.

MEANING AND BEAUTY

Importantly, data and narrative cannot fully describe the world; both rely in some ways on the power of aesthetics (beauty) to complete their task. When a textbook on fish describes a rainbow trout, the observations tend to be technical; when Ernest Hemingway describes a trout, however, the beauty of the fish shines through, providing us with an emotional response rather than merely an intellectual depiction. In the same way, I have rarely met a scientist who did not possess some sort of emotional fascination with the subject of his or her research.

This centrality of beauty to human endeavors cannot be understated. We cannot explain its power or its source, but a story that is lasting and captures our emotional imagination will always outstrip one that is only a matter of curiosity or trivia. In the same way, the technical study of horticulture cannot fully articulate the beauty of flowers. The entire nineteenth-century philosophical and artistic movement called "Romanticism" reacted against the Enlightenment's denuded empiricism.[19] Perhaps this frustration was best articulated by poet William Wordsworth (1770–1850): "The world is too much with us; late and soon, / Getting and spending, we lay waste our powers: / Little we see in Nature that is ours; / We have given our hearts away, a sordid boon! / . . . / For this, for everything, we are out of tune; / It moves us not" ("The World Is Too Much with Us," lines 1–4, 8–9).

Humans have an apparent inborn need for beauty in their lives. This is why we compress narrative into powerful forms that we call "poems." This is why we begin singing at a very early age. This is why the entire crayon industry exists, seeking to satisfy the innate craving that even the youngest children have to create visual art. Stories and poems are not the only beautiful creations of humankind. The very fact that art exists as a specifically human endeavor tells us something else about general revelation.

---

[19]Postmodernism also reacts to the Enlightenment's excesses, including its claims of absolute certainty that are based not on divine revelation but on the affected objectivity of empirical scientism. While Christians tend to read postmodern critiques of objective truth as directed at matters of faith, those same criticisms are also pointed toward secular thinkers who have sought to perform their own version of self-revelation, which is a tepid echo of general revelation.

WHY THE ARTS MATTER: MOVING BEYOND THE WORLD THAT WE KNOW

One of the most specifically human endeavors is artistic expression. From their earliest years, children enjoy drawing, painting, and shaping dough, even as they enjoy poetry, music, and playing dress-up. Cultures around the world engage in artistic endeavors, and from the earliest prehistoric records, they always have. Nowhere in the animal kingdom do we find art like that produced by humans. While we have elephants and monkeys that employ artistic media to produce "art" for fundraisers, these works possess no genuine intentionality that may be documented. Humans, on the other hand, are intrinsically artistic. Apparently we are hardwired for beauty.[20]

THE POWER OF BEAUTY

The philosophical field that deals with beauty is called "aesthetics," which studies the utter diversity of human understandings of the arts. While the definition of beauty is difficult to build into a consensus ("beauty is in the eye of the beholder" sort of just kicks the proverbial can down the road in particularly unhelpful ways), the reality of its importance to human existence is quite clear. What other species decorates its living spaces with purely decorative objects or sings while it works?

Just as words have meaning, the fine arts likewise convey meaning. Beauty points toward a form of transcendence that defies the mundane. Beauty documents that there is something outside of ourselves, something beyond the world that we know. Beauty may be natural or artificial. When we behold a sunset in particular cloud formations over a body of water, we may be dumbfounded

---

[20]For excellent considerations of the fine arts in a Christian context, see Hans Rookmaaker, *Modern Art and the Death of Culture* (Wheaton, IL: Crossway, 1994); Philip Graham Ryken, *Art for God's Sake: A Call to Recover the Arts* (Phillipsburg, NJ: P&R, 2006); Dorothy Sayers, *The Mind of the Maker* (San Francisco: Harper & Row, 1987); Gene Edward Veith Jr., *State of the Arts: From Bezalel to Mapplethorpe* (Wheaton, IL: Crossway, 1991); and Nicholas Wolterstorff, *Art in Action: Toward a Christian Aesthetic* (Grand Rapids, MI: Eerdmans, 1980).

and unable to utter anything more than "Wow!" When we behold the liftoff of a rocket on its way to leaving our atmosphere, we may be struck by the power of the action and find ourselves speechless. When we see the beauty of an infant, we may be unable to avert our stare momentarily. When we find ourselves being pulled into a painting like Rembrandt's *Prodigal Son* or weeping at the sounds of a passage of music, we may find that we are completely over-whelmed with emotion.

The fine arts remind us that this world is not all material. This is why I love that the basic academic organizational unit of most teaching universities is the college of arts and sciences; rightly understood, they are partners, not rivals. They are collaborators, not competitors.

ART AND INTENTIONALITY

All art has a point. It is disingenuous to say that the point is that there is no point, because that is itself a point. The point may be ambiguous or even misleading, but the fact remains that there still is a point. Art's ability to capture reality, however we may define it, in a purely artificial medium such as words or musical notes or pastels is a truly magnificent thing. Indeed, perhaps there is some-thing to the notion that our creative and inventive abilities are a part of the image of God that we bear. Ephesians 2:10 tells us that we are God's *poeia*, not just "workmanship" as the King James Version terms it, but rather that we are his poetry, his artwork, his handicraft.

Because the Scriptures describe God as a craftsman, we would be wise to consider this metaphor as an important insight into the nature of God. Just as he is an author (Heb. 5:9; 12:2) whose words have meaning, he is an architect (Heb. 11:10) whose designs create order for his world. He is a sculptor who built Adam's body (Gen. 2:7) and a skilled artisan who dictates beauty even in the ornamentation of the tabernacle (Exodus 25; note especially the instructions for the ark of the covenant). The Scriptures drip with beauty, both of the natural world and the articles of worship of the Most High God. Beauty points to the supernatural world that lies beyond this realm.

If science prevents us from being foolish, then the arts keep us from losing our humanity through over-attention to the mundane. Beauty reminds us that what is in front of our eyes is not the totality of the world. The Romans had a proverb, *ars longa, tempus breve*, or "art lasts; time is short." Art enhances our perception of time; it preserves the present age for the past. When we tour any city in the world, we find the greatest artworks from past ages continuing to have a voice for new generations. William Shakespeare even proposed that art could grant a kind of immortality:

> But thy eternal summer shall not fade,
> Nor lose possession of that fair thou ow'st,
> Nor shall death brag thou wander'st in his shade,
> When in eternal lines to time thou grow'st,
> So long as men can breathe, or eyes can see,
> So long lives this, and this gives life to thee.[21]

John Keats likewise depicted the ability of art to preserve beauty, declaring in the conclusion of "Ode on a Grecian Urn": "Beauty is truth, truth beauty,—that is all / Ye know on earth, and all ye need to know"[22] (lines 49–50). The ability of the arts to capture time in a form of transcendence that anticipates, however slightly, eternity is a mystery that provides us with an intuitive grasp on the supernatural.

The ability of art to preserve captures glimmers of the truth, providing it with a medium for communicating into the future. Sometimes artistic expressions of truth may outlive the culture that produced the artwork. In our time, Europe is almost completely a

---

[21]William Shakespeare, "Sonnet 18," lines 9–14, in *Sonnets* (New York: Signet, 1964).
[22]John Keats, "Ode on a Grecian Urn," in *The Norton Anthology of English Literature: Major Authors Edition*, 6th ed., ed. M. H. Abrams (New York: Norton, 1966), 1793–95.

post-Christian society; no longer is orthodox faith foundational to those nations that once were leaders in Christendom. Even though this pendulum has swung, one cannot visit a museum, a concert hall, a town square, or a theater anywhere in the Continent without witnessing Christian truth in artistic media. While the people themselves have, unfortunately, lost much of the vocabulary of the gospel, the artifacts that have been left behind provide a bold witness to the power of Christ's service to humankind.

THE BEAUTY OF WONDER

The arts lift up our eyes, our hearts, and our minds to help us move beyond our mundane world and to see that there is something beyond the ordinary. It gives us a glimpse of the world that exists beyond the material universe. It totally distinguishes humans from all other species on the planet. Art grants us a special wonder at the universe that transcends the minutiae of materialistic empiricism.

One of the dangers of an overly rationalistic approach to the world is a loss of this wonder. This leads to a blindness to the aesthetic content that surround us and steals from us the ability to respond to it. I will never forget one of my biology professors talking about plant taxonomy and commenting how everything in botany really looks the same. Roots all pretty much are the same, trunks and stems too, and leaves vary by species but generally share similar morphologies. He declared, "For those of you who believe that God made all of the plants in the world, you certainly do worship a God who lacks a very fertile imagination." Perhaps my professor was the one who lacked imagination or a willingness to acknowledge the beauty and diversity of the plant world.

Imagination is a deeply human trait that derives its abilities from the mind of God. Theologians formerly spoke of God's revealing himself in the book of Scripture and in the book of nature. The latter is a storybook too, one that has meaning and intentionality. The information it contains not only tells the story of how the world functions and works, which may be interpreted through data, but also what the world means in terms of why it functions the way that it does: so that God may be revealed and that his love for creation may be manifested clearly.

6

LIBERAL LEARNING AND THE CORE CURRICULUM

For in him all the fullness of God was pleased to dwell, and
through him to reconcile to himself all things, whether on earth
or in heaven, making peace by the blood of his cross.

—Colossians 1:19–20

Several years ago I spoke with the alumni director of a large state
university about a regular column that appeared in their glossy
biannual publication, which included news and updates. The column allowed former students to write about the faculty members
who had most influenced their lives, and many chose to write not
about the professors who taught them in their major but about
those who taught their general education courses. "It's amazing,"
he said, "how influential those professors tend to be even when the
students take only one course with them!"

That story demonstrates the great irony of the general education curriculum: students tend to treat it as an impediment to
their "real" courses, those in their majors, but the professors who
influence their lives are often those who teach the general courses.
Indeed, many students change their majors after taking core
courses, stumbling across previously unknown talents, interests,
and even passions that end up altering the courses of their lives.

THE CRISIS IN GENERAL EDUCATION

General education courses, also called "core" courses, are sometimes treated like vegetables at a backyard barbecue, tolerated

because they are "good for you." Students pick up on this attitude adroitly, and, in fact, at many campuses, the core curriculum is in a state of crisis. No one seems to be happy with the core. It seems a waste of time for some; others see it as little more than the dead hand of past traditions; for still others, it is an opportunity lost. While "liberal learning is more than general education," as Leon Kass has termed it, the core curriculum is the last, best refuge left on many campuses.[1]

At many institutions, a serious question about the core curriculum has developed: who owns the program? Certainly the academic departments that teach the courses have a stake of ownership, as those courses tend to generate a significant portion of their teaching load as well as student credit hours. The rise of scholarly research as the primary activity of many faculty members, however, has meant that the workload involved in teaching lower-level courses has pushed many full-time faculty members away from those classes. Because of this, temporary faculty (who tend to lack doctoral degrees) or teaching assistants (who have not yet earned graduate degrees) teach the bulk of general education courses. Core courses tend to hold lesser importance. They are "service" courses that are not very important to the lion's share of the faculty.

Ironically, just as questions of ownership have developed, questions of content have intensified as well. Because of the liberal arts' roots in the Western (and Christian) tradition, they are sometimes suspect as a function of sexist, racist, colonialist, and even homophobic belief systems. The stereotypical view of the Western tradition as "dead white males" certainly reigns in some circles. This "hegemony" (authoritarian perspective) of ideas that are no longer fashionable has meant that some scholars work within a system of resentment or even downright "chronological snobbery,"

---

[1]Leon R. Kass, "The Aims of Liberal Education," in *The Aims of Education* (Chicago: University of Chicago Press, 1997), 86.

to use C. S. Lewis's term.[2] These persons argue that there should not be a foundational or restrictive core of knowledge. Sometimes this view is called "multiculturalism" (the belief that all cultures and their expressions are fully equal and that none should be prioritized), or "postmodernism" (the belief that all truth is relative and there is no prioritization of any forms of knowledge as absolute truth), or even "decentralization" (the belief that individuals should not be troubled to master central concepts but should instead be able to determine their own courses of learning).

All these forces have led to general education being a central battleground for intellectual conflicts, some rooted in economics, such as the credentialing of faculty in these courses, and some rooted in academe's more esoteric arguments. In either case, the losers in the process are the students who cannot avail themselves of the intellectual discipleship that may be undertaken in these crucial courses.

Even as these conflicts are playing out, the acute financial difficulties that many campuses face have led to searches for increased economic efficiency in the educational process. The core curriculum is often the easiest place to improve financial margins. By using temporary faculty or teaching assistants, most general education courses bear only half the salary costs of upper-level or graduate courses. Similarly, general education courses typically enroll significantly more students in each section than does an upper-level course. During my senior year, for example, I was among two hundred students in a popular lecture course at the same time as I took a seminar with only three students. Both courses generated the same tuition payment from me, but while one course multiplied that payment by three students, the other multiplied it by hundreds of students, yielding much more revenue for the university. I can only imagine which course the chief financial officer preferred

---

[2] C. S. Lewis, *Surprised by Joy: The Shape of My Early Life* (Boston: Houghton, Mifflin, Harcourt, 1995), 207–8.

that students take (the larger one), just as I can imagine which course a professor would rather teach![3]

Financial concerns have also developed on another front: the decline of traditional four-year undergraduate degrees completed on a particular campus. Very few students complete all of their courses at a single university; they often earn credits elsewhere. Nontraditional universities and programs have grown in size over the past generation, with for-profit institutions, which usually make use of online courses, gobbling up a large share of US students.

Other means for completing college credits have likewise expanded. Credit by examination (through tests like Advanced Placement and CLEP) allows students to bypass many core courses. Additionally, many high schools now offer dual enrollment courses that earn both high school and college credits. Students sometimes earn eighteen to twenty-four college credits before even setting foot on a college campus, which means that they have effectively eliminated their freshman year.[4]

Another practical challenge comes from the change in the structure of college degrees. At one time, undergraduate degrees averaged 128 credit hours, a threshold that has recently moved closer to 120 hours. As that total has declined, professional program requirements have increased from a low of thirty hours to as

---

[3] I would be remiss if I did not note the difference in my educational experience in these two courses. While the large course was very entertaining (the instructor was a fantastic lecturer), I have no memory of a single writing assignment; likewise, I have no memory of being required to read in the text that was assigned. Our tests were completed on computer-scanned grading cards and covered the material from the lectures. In the seminar, which met in the faculty member's office, I had to complete a forty-page research project and a wide range of readings. The difference in the educational outcomes was significant.

[4] This opportunity is part of the reason for the rise in so-called three-year degrees that have been championed by many politicians, such as US Senator Lamar Alexander (TN) in "The Three-Year Solution," *Newsweek* (October 17, 2009), http://www.newsweek.com/2009/10/16/the-three-year-solution.html. These leaders cite the relatively inexpensive costs of courses that lead to credit while students are simultaneously enrolled in secondary schools. Three-year degrees are, in fact, nothing new and have been available for many years; I have written about my own experiences in graduating with my undergraduate degree in 1984 after only three years of coursework: "Confessions of a 3-Year Degree Student," *The Chronicle of Higher Education* (November 4, 2009), http://chronicle.com/article/Confessions-of-a-3-Year-Deg/49001/.

many as sixty; this is particularly true in fields that require licensure (nursing, education, engineering, and business) or those that require extensive apprenticeships (the fine and performing arts). This specialization creates an impediment to an education that provides training in broader critical thinking. In some ways, these kinds of programs risk producing a kind of drone who is narrowly trained and ill-equipped for careers outside of the profession for which he or she has been prepared.

COHERENCE AND COMMONALITY

A traditional approach to liberal learning imparts a common foundational knowledge base with a strong sense of coherence. The reality, however, is that most college core courses operate independently from one another and that the sense of a "grand conversation" never really emerges. Nowhere is the loss of this overarching sense of coherence more lamentable than at the Christian university.

When the core becomes merely a collection of boxes to check off on a curriculum map, it becomes subject to turf battles that may rage with few direct connections to educational ideals. When the courses are not somehow interconnected, students may develop a "silo" mentality, in which they view the courses as totally disposable; once they are over, they can be forgotten.

A Christian approach to liberal learning produces a particularly comely form of learning that is rooted directly in the lordship of Christ as embodied in the pursuit of truth incarnate, for the ultimate glorification of God. Because the gospel is an intellectual statement just as much as it is a spiritual principle,[5] we should not be surprised to find that academic pursuits are particularly fulsome in the light of Christ.

Moreover, where coherence and a gospel focus abound, a

---

[5]The New Testament uses of the words *mind*, *know*, and *truth* make clear just how critical the intellectual life is for Christians.

strong sense of community will prosper all the way down to the level of core courses. If faculty in these various disciplines would converse with one another and engage in team teaching, and if students would participate in cohorts—groups of students taking courses together during a term—these conversations could better filter across campus. Such interactions create a strong sense of relevance across the disciplines.

Co-curricular programs on campus (events and programs sponsored by student life organizations or religious affairs organizations) should have a means of participating in these conversations as well, since most students spend twice the time with these staff members as they do with faculty. Finally, campus chapel programming should be viewed as a first-tier activity that reinforces the work of the core curriculum and grounds this work with specific applications that may be discerned in that context; too many campuses view chapel as an afterthought or a "throw away" hour that is a holdover from past times. Few things energize a Christian campus like an effective chapel speaker whose message resonates with previous discussions in the classroom or spurs subsequent class interactions that are relevant to the topics at hand.

This sense of coherence should also find its way into the financial plan of the university. Core courses must be capped at reasonable sizes so that faculty and students can have the kind of interactions that foster a deeper form of intellectual discipleship that just is not possible in larger lecture courses. Likewise, the overuse of adjuncts and entry-level faculty to the exclusion of permanent faculty is a barrier to the kind of coherence that is possible when the core is viewed as a deeply rooted part of campus life. Certainly a balance must be maintained between these factors and the financial realities of an institution, but care must be taken to protect the important work of core courses as foundational to the university.

If the core provides opportunities for intellectual and spiritual formation or even for the beginning of important mentoring relationships between faculty and students, it might improve student retention and even graduation rates. The institution's mission is played out in its general education program more than, perhaps, any other venue, and reducing it to a merely fiscal understanding is both shortsighted and poor stewardship.

RESTORING THEOLOGICAL FOUNDATIONS

As I mentioned previously, at one time theology was called the "queen of the sciences." One of the great failures of core curricula at many Christian institutions is the confining of theology to chapel programming and a sequence of Old and New Testament courses.

Perhaps some of the hesitancy to tackle theological content in the core curricula is a belief that students possess basic scriptural and doctrinal literacy when they arrive on campus. This belief, however, is undermined by the reality that even the best-educated and most church-saturated students who arrive at Christian institutions tend to lack in-depth knowledge of even the most basic facts of the faith. Surveys and polls all consistently bear this out. The task of theological literacy must be undertaken across campus to ensure that students possess the broadest possible understanding of how their intellectual training may be lived out in their distinctive calling as Christ follower.

Another hesitation to include theological content is the sense of many, if not most, faculty members that they are ill-equipped to lead such discussions. I suspect that this is partially due to the way that professors are trained: they are specialists who know a great deal about a particular subject so are hesitant to hold forth on subjects outside of that field. The stakes of theological discourse are even higher; in the end, many Christian faculty members end up teaching their courses in ways that differ little from their secular counterparts at other universities; they do not teach in distinctively Christian ways that drip with theological content.[6]

No one realistically expects that all faculty members in all academic fields will become experts in theological and biblical exposition, but all faculty members should be actively engaged in pursuing a knowledge of how their discipline is impacted when the lordship of Christ is elevated over all else, including dominant disciplinary presumptions. How do we read literature differently when we view it through the lens of Scripture and biblical hermeneutics? How do we treat issues of justice in sociology differently when we evaluate them in the light of Christ's admonitions for the treatment of our fellow men and women? How do we create and critique art in ways that are influenced by an aesthetic that reflects divine transcendence?

Some faculty members perhaps will complain that this is a burden, but for faculty in religion departments, the burden is even greater, as they must pursue knowledge of all other fields at the university in order to facilitate fruitful conversations among their colleagues. Religion faculty members should model intellectual curiosity that is rooted in theology but conversant with many other academic disciplines. Together, faculty from every discipline can join together as a theologically focused community to model how liberal learning can be lived out in the pursuit of God's calling. In the end, a rigorous core curriculum will cultivate globally engaged, intellectually curious Christ followers.

---

[6]For an excellent overview of this viewpoint, see John E. Hull, "Aiming for Christian Education, Settling for Christians Educating: The Christian School's Replication of a Public School Paradigm," *Christian Scholar's Review* (Winter 2003): 203–24.

7

CURRENT OPPORTUNITIES FOR (AND CHALLENGES TO) LIBERAL LEARNING

Go therefore and make disciples of all nations, baptizing them
in the name of the Father and of the Son and of the Holy Spirit,
teaching them to observe all that I have commanded you.

—Matthew 28:19–20

In 2010 I visited eastern Ukraine, leading in faculty development and teaching English at three universities in the city of Poltava. I had a wonderful week, meeting some of the most gracious hosts imaginable and their eager pupils. As I prepared for my trip, I read up on Ukrainian literary favorites such as Shevchenko, Gogol, and Pushkin, as well as the fascinating history of the nation. I studied the architecture, the distinctive beliefs of the Ukrainian Orthodox Church, the great composers, and a little of the language. I subscribed to an RSS feed for news stories about the country's politics and economics. The last thing I wanted to do when I visited was come across as a cultural bully. I could tell that my hosts were delighted with my many questions about their literature, their history, and their culture. I was humbled by their patience with my many questions.

My preparations reflected my belief in the strength of the liberal learning tradition to prepare one for a task. Because I wanted to be ready for those conversations, I spent a great deal of time in study, poring over everything in English about the Ukrainian church that I could get my hands on. In the wake of my experience, my eyes now have been attenuated to catch all things Ukrainian. My intellectual life has been greatly enhanced by this process of preparation.

For those of us who champion liberal learning, our current era is daunting. Two particular forces seem to undermine the legitimacy of this approach to learning: pragmatism and multicultural relativism. The first tends to denature education into a format that creates human cogs in an economic system, trained to work but not to think. The latter tends to level all things cultural to the point that nothing is exceptional or superior; everything is interchangeable or based on preference. Such interchangeability and preference, however, are distortions of perhaps the best opportunities for liberal learning of the past few centuries.

RECONNECTING VOCATION AND LIBERAL LEARNING

A teacher at an inner-city high school was advising students who were interested in a special program that promoted careers in health care. The teacher encouraged the students to pursue careers as nursing assistants, learning how to assist doctors and nurses in their work. When the students left the room, the teacher's supervisor took her to task for the suggestion: "Stop telling them that they can become nursing aides and start telling them that they can be doctors and nurses instead! There's nothing wrong with being a nursing aide; they are necessary of course, but some of these students need to know that they have the ability and the opportunity to extend their education. Lift up their eyes to opportunities, not just present circumstances."

To some extent this story illustrates the difference between pragmatic educational approaches and more fulsome views of learning. For some, education is merely preparation for a job, producing highly skilled workers for very specific industries or positions. This is sometimes viewed as vocational training, and it is critical to the success of any region, as we need, in all honesty, many more workers who are skilled at these practical tasks. The problem comes, however, when these students are told that all they *ever* will be is technicians, that they do not need to ask larger questions, gain skills as entrepreneurs, or cultivate leadership abilities. This kind of thinking circumscribes the opportunities that such workers may have to start their own businesses, pursue training for other occupations, or even maximize their abilities in nonoccupational pursuits. These then become the workers most at risk for extended unemployment during economic downturns or plant closures. If education is a purely practical pursuit, it becomes something of a blind alley when hard times come.

Nowhere is this view more destructive than in the contemporary emphasis on educational testing. Testing provides accountability, since it measures how effective a teacher has been by analyzing student performance in a particular course. The reverse works as well: students can mark their mastery of the content by their scores on assignments. The problem comes, however, when the test does not assess the content of the course; rather, the course merely prepares students for the examination. In a science class, this means replacing experiments and old-fashioned science-fair projects with focused preparation on the content of the upcoming standardized examinations. Once the exam has been completed, the information may be forgotten, because it has not been connected to any other coursework or future thought. Such a pragmatic approach to education leads immovably toward emptiness and irrelevance.

Unfortunately, the results of pragmatic learning match those of an overly idealistic view of learning as a self-fulfilling process. If knowledge is pursued merely for its own sake, its abstractions remain untethered to application, which is likewise empty and irrelevant. For Christians, this is particularly problematic because the purpose of our learning is the glorification of God. When learning glorifies God, it always yields both truth and application (orthodoxy and orthopraxy). Perhaps this is why Paul warned Timothy against those who are "always learning and never able to arrive at a knowledge of the truth" and are "corrupted in mind and disqualified regarding the faith" (2 Tim. 3:7–8). Both practicality and hyper abstraction have the same net effect: circumscription of effective learning.

In current usage, "vocational training" is equivalent to "practical education," but this is not historically the case. Most Christians have a clear sense of the importance of the term *calling* for their faith. Since I work with college students, I hear this question a great deal: "What is God's calling on my life?" The Latin equivalent to *calling* came through the term *vocare*, "to call," which is the root of the English *vocation*. A truly vocational education is one that understands the role of God's call on our lives, whether we are professional Christians or clergy or lay persons who view the work of our hands as a direct gift from God. From Samuel's "here I am" responses (1 Samuel 3) to Peter's and Andrew's answer to Christ's invitation to follow him (Matt. 4:17–19), the biblical record makes it clear that all Christ followers are to view their lives as dependent on a sensitivity to God's will.

PREPARING FOR A LIFETIME OF LEARNING

Certainly the biblical record shows us the importance of the call to ministry that is dedicated to leading local churches and to missions, but it has been rare indeed in the great expanse of history for those so called to serve exclusively in these roles without having to make a living through another form of employment. Even the apostle Paul continued his tent-making career while serving in his multiple capacities. With the cultural dominance of Christianity, following Constantine's establishment of Christianity as the official public religion, ministry was funded at levels that allowed undistracted service. A definite downside to this development was that the laity became more passive about their roles in the ministries of the church. Indeed, while some are called to special offices, all believers are called to live out their faith with intentionality no matter what their work or family situation might be. All are called, at a minimum, to holy living, and all are commissioned to share the gospel in ways both tangible and specific.

In the West, the history of higher education mirrors, to some extent, the history of the professionalization of Christian ministry. Originally, institutions of higher learning were designed to prepare an educated clergy, but by the late Middle Ages, professional tracks in medicine, law, and other nonclergy fields had developed. Each of these tracks received the foundational liberal arts training, which included a heavy dose of theology and enabled a depth of options for the learned man. Rather famously, Christopher Marlowe's play *Doctor Faustus* (c. 1592) depicts such a man concluding his foundational studies and trying to determine which professional application of that learning might be best for him. He rejects medicine as being doomed to failure (all patients ultimately dying), the law as being too boring, and the clergy as being too tied to a stern God (misreading Romans 6:23).[1] The eventual compartmentalization of Christian service, which accelerated during the Enlightenment, and the increasingly post-Christian culture of the West have left Christendom with an often passive laity that views the work of the church as belonging to the professional clergy.

Our current age is one of transition in how Christians, particularly in the West, view the responsibilities of the faith.

---

[1]Faustus reads Romans 6:23, "For the wages of sin is death," and stops there to declare that this is too hard of a saying. In the Latin Vulgate this passage apparently concludes the printed page, and the reader is required to turn to the next page to read the verse's conclusion: "but the free gift of God is eternal life in Christ Jesus our Lord." Faustus, despite his great learning, is still guilty of being a poor reader, and it changes his eternal destiny, as he rejects Christianity and embraces a diabolical pact.

Increasingly there is a passion among many younger believers to impact the world for Christ in ways that find expression outside of traditional church ministries. Groups of friends are moving into declining neighborhoods to reach out to under-resourced families, individuals are moving to war-torn regions of the world, and young professionals are giving a significant amount of their personal income to support ministries. A number of new strategies portend a new emphasis on an active laity diligently living out its faith in tangible ways.

Indeed, as Western culture is moving into a post-Christian era, where the dominant worldviews of the past millennium become more implicit and suspect, a paradigm is emerging that more closely resembles the Christianity of the first century than that of the nineteenth century. Professional Christians who work solely on church and ministry staffs will become increasingly rare, but this will be matched by a renewed vision of intense and intentional expressions of faith.

A distinctively Christian version of liberal learning will be crucial to the success of these new strategies. Fewer "career" missionaries with theological degrees from seminaries will be commissioned by denominational agencies; rather, engineers and chemists will take positions with corporations that will position them in regions where there is little gospel platform. Full-time church employees who supervise inner-city ministries will become rarer; instead, teachers and social workers will target urban areas as places to build careers so that they may serve populations with particular challenges that may be remediated by the gospel. Business leaders and entrepreneurs will find ways to generate profits in ways that reflect their Christian principles and will fund philanthropic activities through these funds. Church planters will target unreached areas, armed with both theological education and practical platforms, where they will run coffee shops, manage arts agencies, and coach athletics while building relationships that may lead to spiritual transformations in the context of local church fellowships.

A liberal education will be critical to developing the skill sets necessary for success in these kinds of ventures. This will invert the old "Bible college" strategy that dominated the twentieth century. At these institutions, many of which have important legacies of effective preparation for church-based ministries and leadership, all students were expected to major in religion or biblical studies. All other subjects were subordinated to those courses, with few, if any, majors available in the humanities, education, or business. In this configuration, the primary focus was the theological education, which was enhanced by the narrow liberal arts or professional training that was offered.

The time is right for an inversion of this model that hearkens back to the ancient approach to liberal learning: students will prepare for careers in pharmacy, sociology, law, health care, and athletics with expansive liberal arts content, but with a yoking of that training to theological education. In this view, the liberal arts will be rejoined with the former queen of the sciences in ways that specifically equip Christ followers for the good works that lie ahead of them. This liberal learning will prepare them for the platforms that will allow them to be world changers and culture creators and church leaders. Their liberal learning will provide them with a way to glorify God and serve their fellow persons.

PREPARING FOR A GLOBAL SOCIETY

The changes that increasingly affect the church in the United States and in the West more largely also create important opportunities around the world, in both developing nations and in the high-population powerhouses in other regions. The incredible breadth of learning made possible through a distinctively Christian approach to the liberal arts equips students for living in a world that is, as Thomas Friedman so termed it, "flat."[2]

For many persons in the academy, "liberal learning" means "liberal arts," which means "Western tradition." Certainly there are some academic leaders who espouse the absolute primacy of the Western tradition to the exclusion of other cultural traditions. This view perceives cultural traditions on a scale of progress, with the West as the highest form of civilization. Some even hold to a kind of social Darwinistic viewpoint that sees Western culture as more evolved than those found elsewhere in the world.[3] Other champions of the Western tradition are cultural conservatives who fear that we are losing the influence of great thinkers and ideas that have been developed through the three millennia of cultures that have collectively formed the West. Certainly there has been a substantial loss of these influences over the past fifty years. Rare is the student who has read the works of Edmund Spenser, Francis Bacon, or John Milton in the English tradition, and rare as well are those who have actually read Plato, Aristotle, Augustine, Dante, Rousseau, Locke, and so many other thinkers who utterly shaped our own thoughts.

Studying those thinkers is valuable because of their influence on later writers and shapers of history. To illustrate, I wrote my doctoral dissertation on Lady Mary Wroth (c. 1587–1651), the first Englishwoman to publish poetry under her own name. One of my professors asked me if I thought Wroth should be added to the canon of English writers, the first tier of folks who should be read by everyone who takes a literature course. My answer was that as much as I love her poetry (and teach it in my classes), she was an inheritor, not a progenitor, of others. In other words, the influence

---

[2]*The World Is Flat: A Brief History of the Twenty-First Century* (New York: Picador, 2007).
[3]Social Darwinism is the application of classical Darwinism to cultures and their institutions. A fascinating artifact of the perspective of Social Darwinism on global history is H. G. Wells, *The Outline of History: The Whole Story of Man*, 2 vols. (Garden City, NY: Doubleday, 1949), which constantly presumes the evolved superiority of Anglo-European culture.

of her poetry on other writers was minimal. She was worthy of study as a repository of influence but not as a source of influence, which I take to be the foundational qualification for entry into the first tier of the canon of writers. First we study the seminal writers, the fountainheads, then we study others as we build out from those foundations toward other purposes.

Because I have proposed that we view liberal learning through the lens of the Christian intellectual tradition, we will find that the overlap between the Western tradition and this approach is more than slight. Despite contemporary efforts to purge religious thought from intellectual culture, it is impossible to understand Western thought without understanding its religious context. In the same way, it is impossible to understand the Christian intellectual tradition without focusing the largest attention on Western thinkers. These are foundational exercises for educated persons, particularly those who live in the West.

This viewpoint, however, should not be construed as any sort of exclusivist claim for the Western tradition, since it is foundational to the history of ideas, but there are other ideas and traditions that have provided large portions of the world with their intellectual foundations. For someone in the West to connect to, work with, or serve alongside other global cultures, it is critical to study the traditions beyond those of the West. Indeed, if the question of influence is a primary concern for how we construct the content of liberal learning, we must realize that non-Western thought was the primary influence on non-Western cultures.

The rise of global culture has created a philosophical approach that is sometimes called "multicultural relativism," which champions those who either do not live in the West or who note that everyone now shares a global culture, that one demographic group no longer holds absolute dominance over the world of ideas. Perhaps a better term would be *global traditions*, which evokes the interconnectedness we all enjoy because of advances in technology, mobility, and political alliances. Intercultural connections no longer require travel, especially in an immigrant-rich country like the United States. In most cities, one can hear a dozen languages being spoken; even in rural areas, cross-cultural experiences have proliferated over the past few decades. Global traditions represent significant opportunities for those who engage in liberal learning, particularly in a Christian context, no matter where they may live.[4]

Global is increasingly local. For Christ followers, cultural empathy is no longer a value reserved for missionaries who will travel to the ends of the earth. Even as we live and work in our own Jerusalem and Judea, the uttermost parts of the earth are living among us, and it behooves us to be prepared to build relationships with those persons. Cultural empathy is a by-product of classical liberal learning. I often tell my students that one of the reasons Christians should take advantage of liberal learning is that it allows them to communicate effectively with the non-Christian culture that will surround them no matter where they may live. Instead of speaking "Christianese" to non-Christians, we are able to speak their language by understanding their culture. Just as I prepared myself to visit Ukraine, I encourage my students to understand that their liberal learning preparation will one day help them to be able to build relationships with their neighbors from India, their coworkers from Uganda, and their friends from Brazil. For each of those cultural groups, liberal learning provides a portal to a deeper understanding and to more substantial bonds. For the sharing of the gospel, liberal learning helps us to identify points of contact between different cultures and the truth of the Bible, including the identification of the intersection of the DNA

[4]For a helpful overview of the global imperative in missions, see John Piper's *Let the Nations Be Glad: The Supremacy of God in Missions*, 3rd ed. (Grand Rapids, MI: Baker, 2010). For a perspective on the global imperative for Christian higher education, see David S. Dockery, "Thinking Globally about the Future" in *Renewing Minds: Serving Church and Society through Christian Higher Education* (Nashville: Broadman, 2007), 187–206.

of different cultures and the various elements of the gospel that might resonate with particular needs.[5]

This approach is important for larger cultures that transcend political and geographical boundaries as well. Philosophical boundaries may be broken down as well through these kinds of relationships, as secular Western or technological Eastern or animistic folk cultures are met with both genuine relationships and gospel encouragement through the power of liberal learning in a Christian framework. For those who live in a Western context, Western content is of supreme importance, but for other contexts, there may be other cultural markers that are of equal importance. In all cases, however, the methodology of liberal learning is the key to the gate that stands between the different groups.

When we learn *about* something rather than *from* it, we have damned that work or that subject to ultimate irrelevance because we simply place it in an intellectual sack to carry around.[6] Global traditions allow us to learn from and even through liberal learning, establishing it as an effective skill set by which we may prepare ourselves for reaching out to the rest of the world for professional purposes, whether we are travelling or are at home in the United States.

We err when we view liberal learning as a set of content rather than as a methodology with a distinctive set of principles. Such a stance circumscribes the very power that it possesses. Liberal learning, in fact, creates a kind of cultural empathy that is particularly important in a global society. Liberal learners have a marked advantage over pragmatic learners in that they are driven to make connections between ideas that are only possible within the breadth of knowledge that is found in that educational framework.

Not only this, but liberal learners in a Christian context are

[5]See Harry L. Poe's *The Gospel and Its Meaning: A Theology for Evangelism and Church Growth* (Grand Rapids, MI: Zondervan, 1996) for an outstanding exploration of the gospel's many points of contact in different cultures.
[6]Leon R. Kass terms this approach to learning "to think with" others, which develops intellectual empathy. "The Aims of Liberal Education," in *The Aims of Education* (Chicago: University of Chicago Press, 1997), 85.

able to build connections between people as well, viewing education with a relational objective not found in other approaches. This human connectedness is always important to Christians in particular, because of the gospel-focused nature of our lives and callings. Liberal learning allows us to build bridges between cultures and persons in ways that are particularly effective.

At the end of Matthew's Gospel, Christ provides the disciples with what has become known as the Great Commission: "Go therefore and make disciples of all nations, baptizing them in the name of the Father and of the Son and of the Holy Spirit, teaching them to observe all that I have commanded you" (28:19–20); this instruction is reinforced by Christ in Acts 1: "You will be my witnesses in Jerusalem and in all Judea and Samaria, and to the end of the earth" (v. 8). A Christian approach to liberal learning is one of the most effective strategies for preparing to undertake such a vision of a gospel-focused life. It prepares Christ followers for urban settings, for rural settings, for Western living, for non-Western contexts, and for any conceivable path where God's calling might lead.

CONCLUSION

In all my royal dominion people are to tremble and fear before
the God of Daniel, for he is the living God, enduring forever;
his kingdom shall never be destroyed, and his dominion
shall be to the end.

—Daniel 6:26b

One of the first books I can remember reading on my own was a fantastically illustrated life of Daniel from the Old Testament. I still remember the illustrations clearly: the golden statue of the arrogant Babylonian king that everyone had to worship; the look on King Nebuchadnezzar's face as Daniel's three friends were tossed into the fiery furnace for refusing to worship anyone other than God; the flames roaring into the sky, and the look of surprise on the witnesses' faces as they walked out of the fire. I loved the story about how King Darius tossed Daniel into the lions' den, the result of the trickery of those dastardly advisors. The king valued Daniel and ran in the morning to see how his friend had fared. Again, Daniel walked away from the danger.

I suppose I thought of Daniel as a superhero, indestructible because of the protection of Jehovah God. He loved God, adored him even, and though he constantly found blessings from the work of his hands, he likewise found challenges at every turn. I found satisfaction in the way that God demonstrated his power with such clarity.

The fiery furnace was not Daniel's first challenge, though. The first challenge came in the classrooms of the Babylonia University School, where Daniel and his best friends had been taken to learn how to be royal administrators. Daniel 1 describes the institution's admissions requirements: "Youths without blemish, of good appearance and skillful in all wisdom, endowed with knowledge, understanding learning, and competent to stand in the king's palace" (v. 4a). There was only one course of study, the liberal arts, heavy on the humanities: "to teach them the literature and language of the Chaldeans" (v. 4b). This setting was designed to prepare leaders, to acculturate the captive Jewish youths, and to provide fresh blood for the empire's oversight.

Daniel and his friends were devout in their faith. There may be no doubt about this, for they risked their lives to avoid sullying themselves with nonkosher food and drink. The remainder of Daniel 1 describes the examination that was set up for them, a combination physical fitness test (v. 15) and summative inspection of their learning, which the king himself supervised. The young men excelled, and "among all of [the students] none was found like Daniel, Hananiah, Mishael, and Azariah. . . . And in every matter of wisdom and understanding about which the king inquired of them, he found them ten times better than all the magicians and enchanters that were in all his kingdom" (vv. 19–20).

The path to the fiery furnace and the lions' den began in the schoolroom. The faithfulness of the men led not only to these times of further testing but also to the opportunities to lead the empire itself. In Daniel's case in particular, he was the most trusted advisor anywhere. His faith remained strong, even as it served a visible role in his everyday life: "He went to his house where he had windows in his upper chamber open toward Jerusalem. He got down on his knees three times a day and prayed and gave thanks before his God, as he had done previously" (6:10). His opponents hated his piety and had plotted to use it against him, declaring, "We shall not find any ground for complaint against this Daniel unless we find it in connection with the law of his God" (6:5). This is how he ended up in the lions' den.

Daniel's position in the kingdom, though, was specifically linked to God. Daniel possessed an extraordinary work ethic, and his professional conduct was spotless, but the secret to his success came from a unique gift from God himself: "As for these four youths, God gave them learning and skill in all literature and wisdom, and Daniel had understanding in all visions and dreams" (1:17). Daniel was faithful to use the gifts that God had given him: his intellect, his insights, his ability to cultivate trust from persons of power and influence, and in the end his God-empowered liberal learning led the king himself to declare the glory of God:

> I make a decree, that in all my royal dominion people are to tremble and fear before the God of Daniel, for he is the living God, enduring forever; his kingdom shall never be destroyed, and his dominion shall be to the end. He delivers and rescues; he works signs and wonders in heaven and on earth, he who has saved Daniel from the power of the lions. (6:26–27)

From the lips and the pen of a pagan dictator came words of praise for God, all because of Daniel's fearless use of his academic gifts.

Daniel's story mirrors that of Moses as well. Moses learned all of the great wisdom and knowledge of Egypt, which prepared him to lead the Israelites during the exodus. The tutelage of his liberal learning specifically allowed God to use him for his purposes. In the New Testament, Saul was a similar case, a young man who had excelled in school and whose learning was apparently so broad that, after his conversion and name change, Paul could enter into Athens, to the very heart of Greek learning, and hold his own at Mars Hill with the greatest thinkers of his day. This is the same story with Augustine, and C. S. Lewis, and so many other influential persons within the Christian intellectual tradition. In every case, history was changed because they anticipated the words of Romans 12:2, "Do not be conformed to this world, but be transformed by the renewal of your mind, that by testing you may discern what is the will of God, what is good and accept-able and perfect."

The Christian intellectual tradition is not always recognized with the respect it deserves in today's academic culture. Christian thought and principles are not always held in the highest esteem. Christian voices are not always welcomed at the table of ideas. Sometimes students are frustrated by this, even as leaders are often stymied by misperceptions or outright lies about their work and beliefs. Contemporary culture is increasingly hostile toward per-sons of faith.

Singer-songwriter Michael Card tells about some sage advice he received from his mentor William Lane when confronted with an unfair situation: "Let excellence be your protest." This is out-standing counsel for any Christian who finds herself in a difficult spot. When we allow excellence to be our protest, we will be gra-cious even to those who treat us unfairly. When we allow excellence to be our protest, we will work harder than anyone else. When we allow excellence to be our protest, we will rely on God to open doors for us, trusting him to vindicate us, even if that vindication does not come in this life. How can we not be excellent when we serve the God of the universe?

The Gospel of John makes an almost offhand comment about Jesus's dealing with the apostle Philip when preparing to feed the multitudes. Jesus apparently asked questions about the crowd knowing the answer but preparing the disciples to dis-cern the point of the impending miracle: "[Christ] himself knew what he would do" (6:6b). A fiction writer would call this fore-shadowing, which adds dramatic irony to the passage. While the comment is tied specifically to the miracle of the feeding, it is a warm reminder that God has planned out every step of his redemptive story for all of humankind and plants clues for us to discover, in hindsight, his marvelous plan to reveal himself. In a general sense, though, he has revealed himself to us through nature and our own human nature. He has provided us with his written Word to guide us. We can focus these generalities down to a more personal nature, though. Because he loves us, he reveals himself to each of us as well. And through the medium of liberal learning that places its foundation in his self-revelation, he equips each of us for every good work, work that will bring glory to him.

QUESTIONS FOR REFLECTION

1) Why is it important to maintain a link between general revelation and special revelation? What happens if we disconnect those two concepts?

2) Liberal learning proposes that we become lifelong learners instead of merely preparing for a single employment opportunity. Why is this important?

3) In what ways does liberal learning expand a person's approach to thinking? Similarly, in what ways do narrower approaches to education limit a person's thoughts?

4) How does the lordship of Christ influence how we define the way we pursue education? What does a devotional approach to learning look like in your educational activities?

5) How can we find the right balance between Christian and non-Christian approaches to education? What resources and traditions can guide us in this?

GLOSSARY

Aesthetics. The study of beauty and its relationship with human culture, typically applied to the fine and performing arts.

Christian intellectual tradition. The expansive community of thinkers that spans all centuries since Christ and includes all academic disciplines in producing scholarship that describes the world and humanity's place in it through the lens of orthodox theology.

Core curriculum. Also called "general education," the set of courses that most colleges and universities assign to all students, providing them with a common or "core" set of experiences.

Cultural empathy. Sensitivity to other cultures that seeks to build relationships among people and is facilitated by the application of liberal learning to cultures alien to the learner.

Data hermeneutics. Similar to the hermeneutics of text, data hermeneutics explores how observer bias and presuppositions influence how scientific data are interpreted.

Education. The process of passing intellectual, spiritual, and cultural values across generations.

General revelation. The theological proposition that God has revealed himself to humankind through the created world, allowing even those who do not have full or special revelation (Christ or the Scriptures) to have insights about the nature and person of God.

Global traditions. The interconnectedness of cultures from around the world that is facilitated by technology, ease of travel, and significant immigration opportunities.

Hermeneutics. Formal approaches to interpreting texts, particularly the Scriptures, by attempting to connect the author's meaning with the perceived meaning of the reader.

Intentional fallacy. In hermeneutics, the belief that the writer's intent for a written work is irrelevant because it is outside the text. This shifts the authority over a text's meaning from the writer to the reader.

Liberal learning. An educational approach that emphasizes well-rounded foundational study in the arts and sciences, building on the ancient traditions of the trivium and the quadrivium.

Multicultural relativism. The view that no culture is superior to any other culture, so all cultures are relatively equal even in the area of ethics, and no one can claim that any culture's values are faulty.

Narrative. Stories that are told to describe human experiences.

Postmodernism. The philosophical movement in many academic disciplines away from the modern explanations of the world, including the existence of objective truth and transcendent meaning.

Pragmatism. The philosophical school of thought that elevates the practical and the immediate as the highest good, over (and sometimes against) other considerations, including morality.

Proofs. Mathematical analyses of problems that produce consistent results; proofs may be built upon to provide further proofs, establishing an efficient methodology for exploring the universe.

Quadrivium. In the traditional liberal arts, the four subjects (arithmetic, astronomy, music, and geometry) that built on the trivium to describe how the universe is ordered and functions.

Scientific materialism. The philosophical school of thought that because the material world is the only part of the universe that may be measured, it is the only realm of objective knowledge. This view elevates the scientific method as the "gold standard" for describing truth and reality to the exclusion of all other means of interpreting the world.

Social Darwinism. The application of Charles Darwin's survival of the fittest to human cultures, proposing that some cultures are more advanced than others and that they should be allowed to hold authority over cultures that are less sophisticated.

Solipsism. The belief that the only thing we may know with any certainty is the existence of our individual minds. Taken to the extreme, this view proposes that only the individual exists and all of reality is the invention of one's own mind.

Special revelation. The theological proposition that God has revealed himself most fully through the incarnation of Christ and through the documentation of God's story in the Scriptures. Special revelation is a lens through which general revelation may best be understood.

Trivium. In the traditional liberal arts, the three subjects (grammar, rhetoric, and logic) that provide foundational study for latter subjects. The trivium prepared students to grasp the prudent use of language to communicate with others.

RESOURCES FOR FURTHER STUDY

Blamires, Harry. *The Christian Mind: How Should a Christian Think?* Vancouver, BC: Regent College Publishing, 2005.

Cahill, Thomas. *How the Irish Saved the Civilization: The Untold Story of Ireland's Heroic Role from the Fall of Rome to the Rise of Medieval Europe.* New York: Anchor, 1995.

Dockery, David S., ed. *Faith and Learning: A Handbook for Christian Higher Education.* Nashville: Broadman, 2012.

————. *Renewing Minds: Serving Church and Society through Christian Higher Education.* Nashville: Broadman, 2007.

Green, Bradley G. *The Gospel and the Mind: Recovering and Shaping the Intellectual Life.* Wheaton, IL: Crossway, 2010.

Howell, Russell W. *Mathematics through the Eyes of Faith.* New York: HarperOne, 2011.

Kass, Leon R. "The Aims of Liberal Education." In *The Aims of Education.* Edited by John Boyer. Chicago: University of Chicago Press, 1997.

Keller, Timothy. *The Reason for God: Belief in an Age of Skepticism.* New York: Dutton, 2008.

Kuyper, Abraham. *Wisdom and Wonder: Common Grace in Science and Art.* Translated by Nelson D. Kloosterman. Edited by Jordan J. Ballor and Stephen J. Grabill. Grand Rapids, MI: Christian's Library Press, 2011.

Lewis, C. S. *The Abolition of Man, or Reflections on Education with Special Reference to the Teaching of English in the Upper Forms of Schools.* San Francisco: HarperSanFrancisco, 1974.

————. *Mere Christianity.* London: Collins, 1952.

Markos, Louis. *From Achilles to Christ: Why Christians Should Read the Pagan Classics.* Downers Grove, IL: InterVarsity Academic, 2007.

Marsden, George M. *The Soul of the American University: From Protestant Establishment to Established Non-Belief.* New York: Oxford University Press, 1996.

Morris, Tim, and Don Petcher, *Science and Grace: God's Reign in the Natural Sciences.* Wheaton, IL: Crossway, 2006.

Newman, John Henry. *The Idea of a University.* South Bend, IN: Notre Dame University Press, 1982.

Riesen, Richard A. *Piety and Philosophy: A Primer for Christian Schools.* Ozark, AL: ACW Press, 2002.

Rookmaaker, Hans. *Modern Art and the Death of Culture.* Wheaton, IL: Crossway, 1994.

Ryken, Philip Graham. *Art for God's Sake: A Call to Recover the Arts.* Phillipsburg, NJ: P&R, 2006.

Samson, Philip J. *6 Modern Myths about Christianity and Western Civilization.* Downers Grove, IL: InterVarsity, 2001.

Sayers, Dorothy. *The Mind of the Maker.* San Francisco: Harper & Row, 1987.

Sire, James W. *Habits of the Mind: Intellectual Life as Christian Calling.* Downers Grove, IL: InterVarsity, 2000.

Veith, Gene Edward, Jr. *State of the Arts: From Bezalel to Mapplethorpe.* Wheaton, IL: Crossway, 1991.

Wiker, Benjamin, and Jonathan Witt, *A Meaningful World: How the Arts and Sciences Reveal the Genius of Nature.* Downers Grove, IL: IVP Academic, 2006.

Wolterstorff, Nicholas. *Art in Action: Toward a Christian Aesthetic.* Grand Rapids, MI: Eerdmans, 1980.

CONSULTING EDITORS

Hunter Baker
Timothy George
Niel Nielson
Philip G. Ryken
Michael J. Wilkins
John D. Woodbridge

INDEX

✚ CHECK OUT THE OTHER BOOKS IN THE
**RECLAIMING THE CHRISTIAN
INTELLECTUAL TRADITION SERIES**

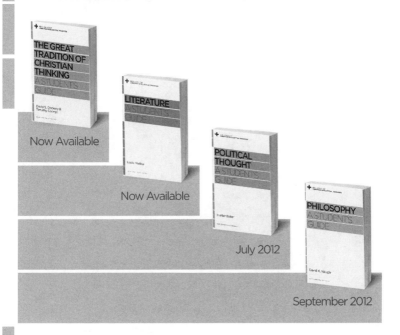

Now Available

Now Available

July 2012

September 2012